Olympiad Champs

ENGLISH

CLASS 2

with **Chapter-wise Previous 10 Year** (2013 - 2022) Questions

DISHA™
Publication Inc

DISHA Publications Inc.

45, 2nd Floor, Maharishi Dayanand Marg,
Corner Market, Malviya Nagar, new Delhi –110017
Tel: 49842349/ 49842350

Typeset By

DISHA DTP Team

Buying books from DISHA

Just Got A Lot More Rewarding!!!

We at DISHA Publication, value your feedback immensely and to show our apperciation of our reviewers, we have launched a review contest.

To participate in this reward scheme, just follow these quick and simple steps:
- Write a review of the product you purchase on Amazon/Flipkart.
- Take a screenshot/photo of your review.
- Mail it to *disha-rewards@aiets.co.in*, along with all your details.

Each month, selected reviewers will win exciting gifts from DISHA Publication. Note that the rewards for each month will be declared in the first week of next month on our website.

https://bit.ly/review-reward-disha.

Write To Us At

feedback_disha@aiets.co.in

Preface

We are pleased to launch the 4th edition of **Olympiad Champs English Class 2** which is the first of its kind book on Olympiad in many ways.

The Unique Selling Proposition of this new edition is the inclusion of past year questions till 2022 of different Olympiad exams held in schools.

The book is aimed at achieving not only success but deep rooted learning in children. It is prepared on content based on National Curriculum Framework prescribed by NCERT. All the text books, syllabi and teaching practices within the education programme in India must follow NCF. Hence, Olympiad Champs become an ideal book not only for the Olympiad Exams but also for strengthening the concepts for Class 2.

There is an exhaustive range of thought provoking questions in MCQ format to test the student's knowledge thoroughly. The questions are designed so as to test the knowledge, comprehension, evaluation, analytical and application skills. Solutions and explanations are provided for all questions. The questions are divided into two levels-Level 1 and Level 2. The first level, Level 1, is the beginner's level which comprises of questions like fillers, analogy and odd one out. When the child covers Level 1, it means his basic knowledge about the subject is clear and now it is ready for Level 2. The second level is the advanced level. Level 2 comprises of techniques like matching, chronological sequencing, picture, passage and feature based, statement correct/ incorrect, integer based, puzzle, grid based, crossword, venn diagram, table/ chart based and much more.

The first concern which each parent faces is how to make their children read a book especially when it is based on academics. Keeping this in mind interesting facts, real life examples, historical preview, short cut to problem solving, charts, diagrams, illustrations and poems are added. In addition to this, we have introduced comic strip which increases the readability quotient and make the reading experience for the children more exciting.

With the vision to remove all the misconception a child may have pertaining to the subject, to relate his knowledge to the real world and to develop a deeper understanding of the subject this book will cater all the requirements of the students who are going to appear in Olympiads.

While preparing this book, some errors might have crept in. We request our readers to identify those errors and send it across on **feedback_disha@aiets.co.in.**

We wish you all the best for your Olympiads and happy reading.......

Team Disha

For feedback : feedback_disha@aiets.co.in.

CONTENTS

Unlock your child's
HIDDEN GENIUS!
with Olympiad Champs

DISHA
Publication Inc

10 Principles to CRACK ANY EXAM

1. Chase consistency, not intensity.

Doing intensive study makes your day. But it also exhausts you in the long run, leading to lesser output and added pressure. Toppers always focus on doing consistent work daily, for consistency is far more valuable than intensity.

Remember consistent study of 4 hours every day is more important and powerful than studying 12 hours a day and then not studying at all for next 2 days.

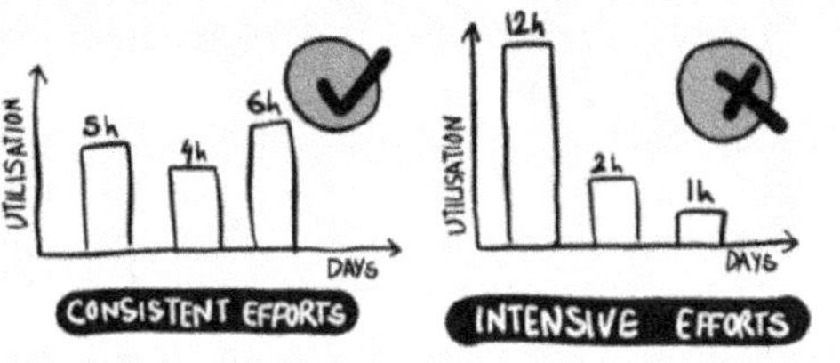

2. Go beyond the surface.

Most students only see a few reasons (teacher, coaching, books, etc) behind Toppers' success, which is only the tip of the iceberg. What they donot see is Toppers Mindset, self belief, habits and discipline and that is where the real problem is.

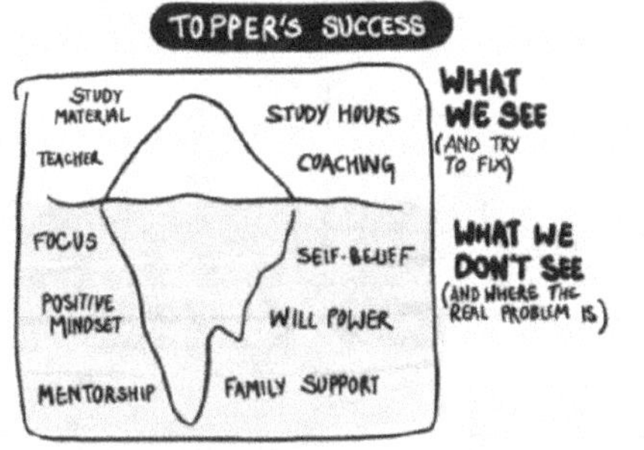

3. Focus on giving your best, not chasing the best.

We want the best coaching, the best teacher, best batch and the best books but we are not ready to give our BEST. Success comes only when we are ready to give our best. We must focus on giving our best than chasing excuses to cover up our failures.

4. Clarity of concept is the key

Concept clarity is critical. If you cannot solve a question, you must go back to the theory and thoroughly examine the concept instead of referring to the solutions. Remember question is one of the chehra(face) of the concept. When toppers get stuck in a problem, they go back and refer the theory(read the concept again and again on which the question is based)

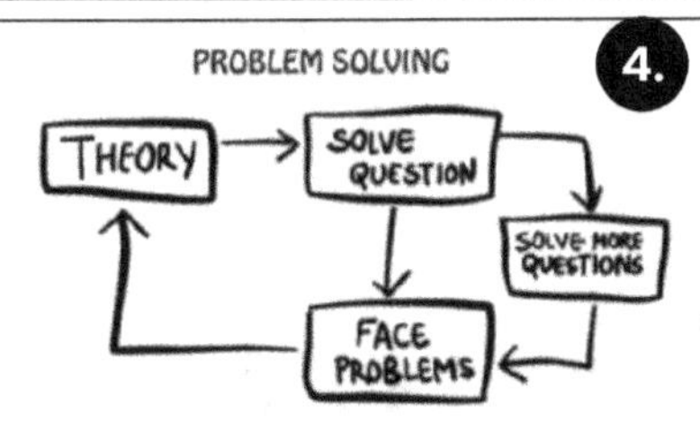

5. Every failure should be a lesson learned.

Most students do not learn from their failures and repeat their mistakes. Toppers also face failures, but they learn from mistakes and elevate themselves. Making mistakes and learning from them is the key to success.

6. Choosing the quality of resources is more important than quantity.

More than 90% of the questions in most books are the same as their substitutes. Instead of practicing from four books and failing to complete them, it is best to prepare from two books and complete them with thorough revisions.

7. Difficult things become easy by taking it one day at a time.

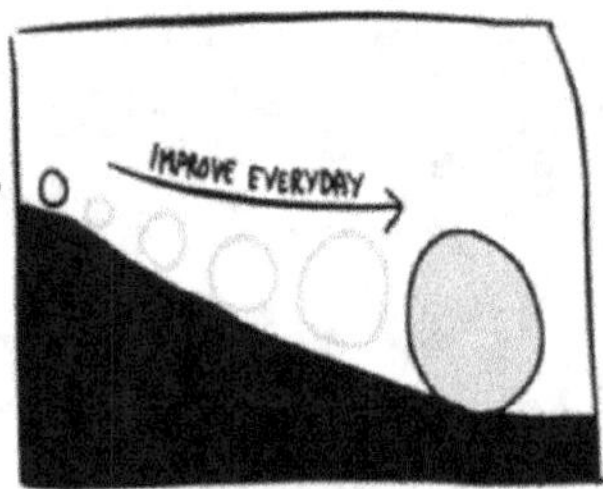

The best way to take any preparation forward is by taking it one day at a time. It makes the impossible possible by taking small steps every day.

Starting a difficult subject. No worries. Keep on working session by session, day by day and week by week and one day you will become unstoppable force.

8. Everything is easy

Before starting everything looks difficult. Once you take a first step, it slowly starts looking easy and over a period of time you become master in the activity. This is toppers secret to become master in any subject.

9. Nobody is gifted

We think toppers are god gifted. We think toppers have high IQ. We think toppers are special/lucky. But the truth is every topper was once an average student(no body is born topper). What makes them different is their consistent and focused efforts

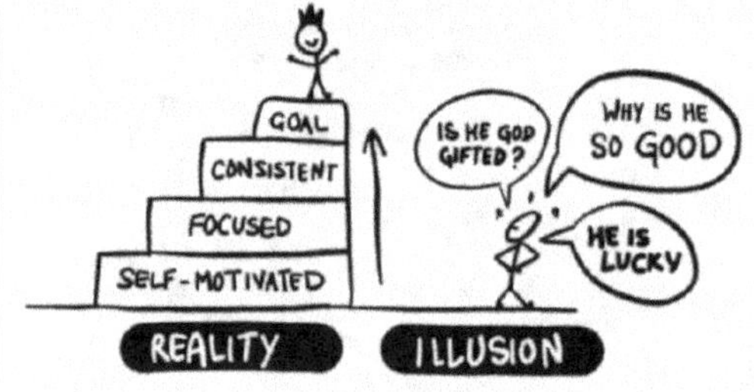

10. Believe in your journey and success will come to you.

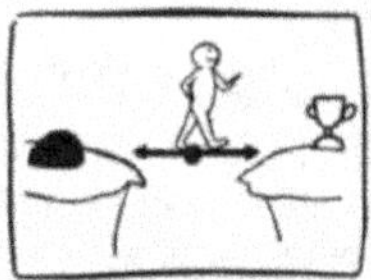

There is never a straight path to success; hard work & patience is required for the results to show up. Keep on working hard without thinking too much about the results and success will come to you eventually.

1 | CHAPTER FOREWORD

Kids! you will notice that all the things around you have a name. In this chapter, you will know about naming words, known as nouns.

Here is an activity for you, based on name of places and things.

Directions : Make a word chain. The new word is made with the last letter of the old word.

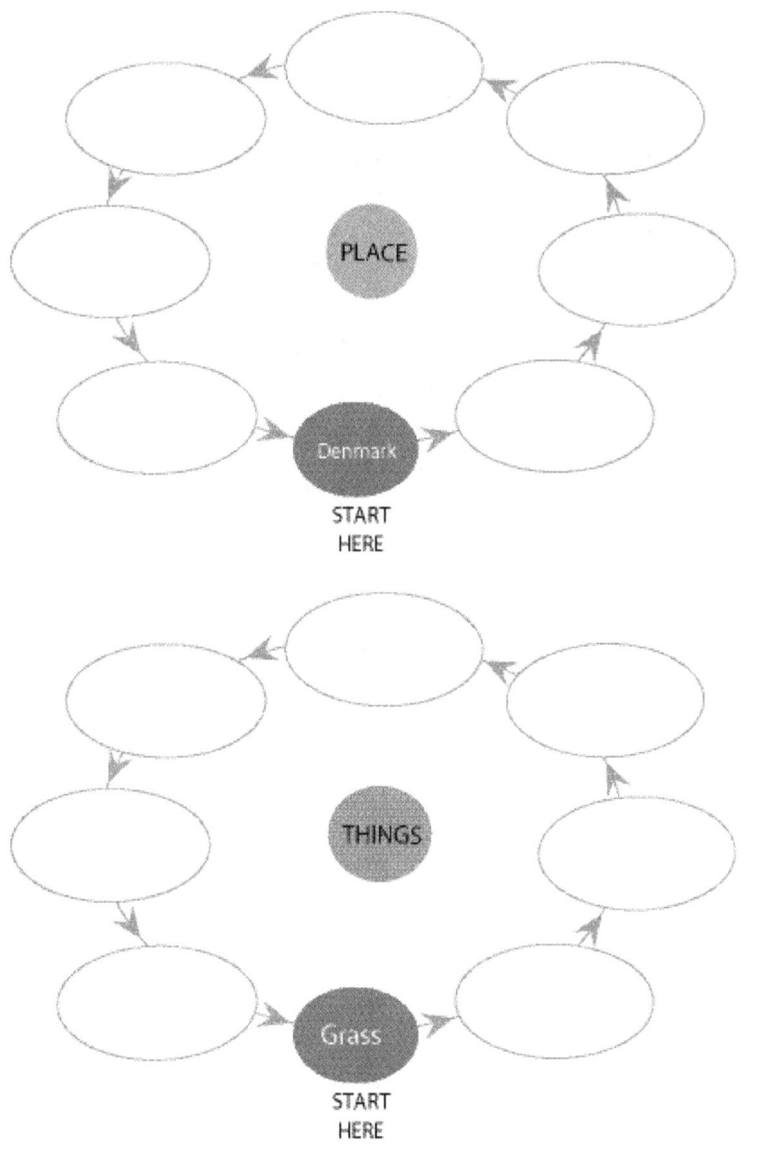

Nouns

LEARNING OBJECTIVES

This lesson will help you to

- understand nouns as naming words
- understand different types of nouns.

INTRODUCTION

Nouns are naming words. The name of a person, place or thing is called a noun. Everything around us has a name, like the Chair you sit upon, or a place that you go to study, is known as a school.

Chair

School

Common Nouns: Names given to a class of things around you like dog, cat, school, mat etc. are called common nouns.

Dog

Cat

Proper Nouns: Names given to people, countries, cities, lanes, rivers, months, days, pets are called proper nouns. Proper nouns always start with a capital letter.

For example: India, Qutub Minar.

Qutub Minar   India

Collective Nouns: Nouns that tell us about a group of things' people or animals are called collective nouns.

For example: A bouquet of flowers, A flight of steps

A bouquet of flowers   A flight of steps

SOME COLLECTIVE NOUNS

Flower	A bouquet of flowers
Steps	A flight of steps
Cards	A deck of cards
Ships	A fleet of ships
Lion	A pride of lions
Elephant	A herd of elephants
Students	A Class of students
Players	A team of players
Monkeys	A troop of monkeys
Birds	A flock of birds
People	A crowd of people
Fish	A school or shoal of fisher
Bees	A swarm of bees
Stamps	A collection of stamps.

Singular Nouns: Singular nouns refer to single things.
For example : A flower, A box.

A flower   A box

Do you know

1. A dog lives in a **kennel**.
2. A horse lives in a **stable**.
3. A lion lives in **den**.
4. A rabbit lives in a **burrow**.
5. A spider lives in a **web**.

Plural Nouns refer to things that are more than one in number.

Rules to change into plural noun.

1. (a) Ba<u>by</u>   → Bab<u>ies</u>

    (Consonant + y)

   (b) BO<u>Y</u>   → Bo<u>ys</u>

    (Vowel + y)

For example : 'Baby' can be changed to 'Babies'.

A baby   Babies

2. (a) Wol<u>f</u>   → Wol<u>ves</u>
    (b) Kni<u>fe</u>   → Kni<u>ves</u>
    * Change f,fe to <u>ves</u>

For example: 'Wolf' becomes 'Wolves'.

A wolf   Wolves

3. Add 'es' if the countable noun ends with sh, ch,x, s

    e.g.

    Ben<u>ch</u> – Benche<u>s</u>
    Bo<u>x</u>   – Box<u>es</u>
    Bru<u>sh</u> – Brushe<u>s</u>
    Bu<u>s</u>   – Bus<u>es</u>

For example: 'Box' becomes 'boxes'.

A box   Boxes

Plural Possessive Nouns: Plural possessive nouns tell us about ownership by more than one person like Boys' books, Girls' room.

Countable Nouns: A noun is countable if <u>it can be counted</u> like <u>one biscuit, two biscuits</u>. Countable nouns can be singular as well as plural.

Uncountable Nouns: A noun is uncountable if it <u>cannot be counted</u> like <u>sand, salt, sugar</u>. They cannot be changed to plural.

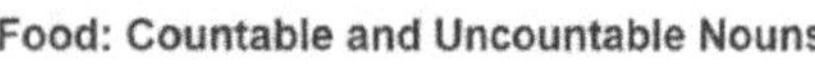

Food: Countable and Uncountable Nouns

Uncountable nouns cannot be counted in number but we can measure them using other units like, Litre, Kilogram, etc.

Sugar

Oil

Masculine Nouns: A noun is a masculine gender if it denotes a male like father, son, uncle, brother.

A man

A boy

Feminine Nouns: A noun is a feminine gender if it denotes a female like mother , daughter, girl, sister, aunty.

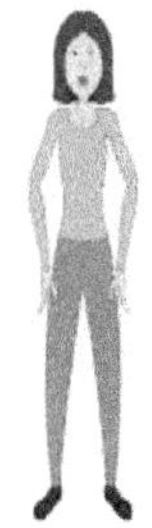

A woman

A girl

Neuter Gender: A noun that denotes a lifeless thing like pencil, book, computer.

A pencil

A car

Multiple Choice Questions

LEVEL – 1

Directions (Qs. 1–5): Look at the pictures and choose the right word from the options given below.

1. (a) Aeroplane   (b) Helicopter   (c) Bus   (d) Truck

2. (a) Cricket   (b) Baseball   (c) Basketball   (d) Hockey

3. (a) Rain   (b) Rainbow   (c) Sky   (d) Umbrella

4. (a) Tree   (b) Plant   (c) Creeper   (d) Climber

5. (a) Baseball   (b) Basketball   (c) Tennis   (d) Golf

Directions (Qs. 6–10) : Look at the pictures and choose the correct option.

6. Flower   (2016)

 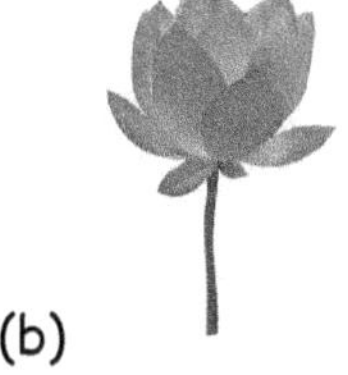  

(a)   (b)   (c)   (d)

7. Leopard

(a)   (b)   (c)   (d)

8. Shoes

  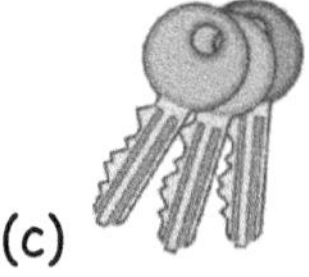 

(a)   (b)   (c)   (d)

9. Taj Mahal   (2015)

(a)   (b)   (c)   (d)

10. Mr. Narendra Modi

(a)   (b)   (c)   (d)

Directions (Qs. 11-15) : Read the questions and choose the correct option.

11. Which of the following is a proper noun?
    (a) Christmas   (b) Boy   (c) School   (d) Books

12. Complete the sentence using a common noun?   **(2013)**
    Jack and Jill went up the ___________.
    (a) circus   (b) school   (c) Mount Everest (d) hill

13. Which of the following is a countable noun?
    (a) Sand   (b) Box   (c) Sugar   (d) Milk

14. Can you please give me ___________ sugar?
    (a) much   (b) many   (c) some   (d) glass

15. Give the plural of story.
    (a) Storys   (b) Stories   (c) Story   (d) Storyes

Directions (Qs. 16-20) : Read the questions and choose the correct option.

16. Identify the 'masculine gender'.
    (a) Women   (b) Uncle   (c) Lady   (d) Sister

17. Identify the neuter gender.   **(2014)**
    (a) Computer   (b) Girl   (c) Boy   (d) Son

18. Identify the 'Feminine gender'.
    (a)   (b)   (c)   (d)

19. Identify the plural of
    (a)   (b)   (c)   (d) None

20. A dog lives in a ________.   **(2017)**
    (a) shed   (b) farm   (c) house   (d) kennel

21. Where can you not listen to music ?   **(2018)**
    (a) Bedroom   (b) Park   (c) Library   (d) Kitchen

22. Which is not natural ?   **(2018)**
    (a) Rain   (b) Plastic   (c) Forest   (d) Beach

23. What is a baby cow called ?   **(2019)**
    (a) Hogget   (b) Lamb   (c) Bull   (d) Calf

24. Which is not made with plastic ? (2019)

(a) Cups   (b) Computers   (c) Powder   (d) None of these

25. Identify the word which is not a noun. (2020)

(a) Terrific
(b) Telephone
(c) Taxi
(d) Television

> **Example**
> Which animal does not have legs
> (a) Horse   (b) (Fish)
> (c) Cat   (d) Dog

26. The boy is playing a ________. (2022)

(a) flute   (b) drum   (c) guitar   (d) piano

LEVEL - 2

Directions (Qs. 1–4): Read the passage and fill in the blanks from the options given below. [Tricky]

Many ________(1) fall sick in winter. It all happens as they do not take proper care. They do not want to wear ______(2). They walk barefoot. Without even wearing____(3). They suffer from cold and cough. The ______(4) should take proper care during winters.

1. (a) pictures   (b) cycles   (c) plants   (d) children
2. (a) sweaters   (b) pillows   (c) bags   (d) books
3. (a) shoes   (b) socks   (c) slippers   (d) pens
4. (a) bags   (b) children   (c) trees   (d) pens
5. **Why, do you think we should wear proper clothes in winters?**
   (a) Because they protect us from falling sick
   (b) Because they make you look beautiful
   (c) Because we can buy many clothes
   (d) No, we should wear proper clothes as they make us look fat.

Directions (Qs. 6–10): Fill in the blanks with the collective nouns.

6. **My mother gave me a ______ of flowers.** (2013)

(a) bunch   (b) branch   (c) bouquet   (d) brunch

7. Has someone seen a _______ of lions?

    (a) herd   (b) pride   (c) group   (d) troop

8. Go left, and then you will see a ________ of steps.

    (a) number   (b) many   (c) flight   (d) collection

9. We saw a ______ of fish swimming in shallow water.   (2016)

    (a) herd   (b) shoal   (c) group   (d) troop

10. There was a _____ of monkeys swinging on the trees.

    (a) pride   (b) herd   (c) troop   (d) litter

Directions (Qs. 11–14): Read the sentences carefully and choose the Uncountable nouns from the options given below.

11. He went to beach and played with sand.   (2017)

    (a) He   (b) beach   (c) played   (d) sand

12. He spent all his money, while shopping.   (2016)

    (a) all   (b) spent   (c) money   (d) shopping

13. The grass is always greener on the other side

    (a) grass   (b) greener   (c) other   (d) side

14. I had very long hair.

    (a) I   (b) had   (c) long   (d) hair

Directions (Qs. 15–19): Read the sentences given below and choose the plural form of underlined nouns from the options given below.

15. The <u>thief</u> entered our house from the back door

    (a) thiefs   (b) thieves   (c) theives   (d) theef

16. The <u>wolf</u> fooled the lion.   (2015)

    (a) wolves   (b) wolfs   (c) wolfes   (d) wolve

17. They cut the fruits with <u>knife</u>.

    (a) knifes   (b) knives   (c) kneves   (d) knifs

18. I saw <u>monkey</u> snatching away food from people.

    (a) monkies   (b) monkeys   (c) monkys   (d) monkyies

19. The <u>baby</u> wanted to go out.

    (a) babies   (b) babys   (c) babyes   (d) babyies

Directions (Qs. 20–24): Read the sentences carefully and choose the proper nouns. Choose the answers from the options given below.

20. Ram is my best friend. We always help each other.   (2014)

    (a) Ram   (b) best   (c) friend   (d) help

21. This is my bicycle. I bought it from Tinkle cycles.

    (a) Bicycle   (b) bought   (c) Tinkle   (d) cycles

22. I went to America last year.
    (a) went   (b) America   (c) last   (d) year
23. My Mom's name is Rekha. She cooks very good food.   (2016)
    (a) Mom   (b) Rekha   (c) She   (d) cooks
24. January is the first month of the year.
    (a) first   (b) month   (c) January   (d) year

Directions (Qs. 25–29): Read the questions and choose the correct option.

25. Which noun in Bold print names a person?   (2016)
    (a) The **Sun** shines.   (b) The **sand** is hot.
    (c) **Tia** jumps into water.   (d) The **water** feels cool.
26. Which noun in Bold print names an animal, a place or a thing?   (2016)
    (a) The **runners** lined up.   (b) The **people** cheered.
    (c) The **sister** ran fast.   (d) She won a gold **medal**.
27. Which word in Bold print is a noun?   (2015)
    Newborn baby kangaroos **are smaller** than **your thumb**.
    (a) are   (b) smaller   (c) your   (d) thumb
28. 'Mare-choose the gender.
    (a) Masculine   (b) Feminine   (c) Neuter   (d) None
29. We wear a ______________ to school.
    (a) dress   (b) uniform   (c) saree   (d) pajamas

Direction (Q. 30): Look at the grid and tell the name of months. Choose the answer from the options given below.   **(Critical Thinking)**

j	u	l	y	a
u	a	m	k	u
n	p	a	t	g
e	r	r	m	u
k	i	c	n	s
o	l	h	b	t
m	o	h	n	t

30. (a) january, february, march, april, june
    (b) april, march, june, july, , august
    (c) april, march, september, november
    (d) june, august, september, october.

Directions (Qs. 31 - 34): Read the following sentences and replace the underlined words with their plurals from the options given below

31. He came and ate the <u>sweet</u> from the box.
    (a) sweetes   (b) sweats   (c) sweets   (d) sweyetes

32. My house is near the <u>church</u>.
    (a) churchs   (b) churchess   (c) churchees   (d) churches

33. His father drops him to <u>school</u> every day.

    (a)   schoals   (b)   schooles

    (c)   schooless   (d)   schools

34. Keep these books in the <u>shelf</u>.

    (a)   shelfs   (b)   shelfes   (c)   shelvs   (d)   shelves

35. What kind of an animal has no hair ?   **(2019)**

    (a) Cow   (b) Dog   (c) Eel   (d) Tiger

36. Where can you not fly a kite ?   **(2019)**

    (a) Cliff   (b) Garden   (c) Hillside   (d) Lounge

37. Which of these you cannot drink?   **(2020)**

    (a) Juice   (b) Coffee   (c) Tea   (d) Salad

38. What is a baby deer called?   **(2020)**

    (a) Pup   (b) Fawn   (c) Puggle   (d) Infant

RESPONSE GRID

LEVEL 1

1. a b c d   2. a b c d   3. a b c d   4. a b c d   5. a b c d

6. a b c d   7. a b c d   8. a b c d   9. a b c d   10. a b c d

11. a b c d   12. a b c d   13. a b c d   14. a b c d   15. a b c d

16. a b c d   17. a b c d   18. a b c d   19. a b c d   20. a b c d

21. a b c d   22. a b c d   23. a b c d   24. a b c d   25. a b c d

26. a b c d

LEVEL 2

1. a b c d   2. a b c d   3. a b c d   4. a b c d   5. a b c d

6. a b c d   7. a b c d   8. a b c d   9. a b c d   10. a b c d

11. a b c d   12. a b c d   13. a b c d   14. a b c d   15. a b c d

16. a b c d   17. a b c d   18. a b c d   19. a b c d   20. a b c d

21. a b c d   22. a b c d   23. a b c d   24. a b c d   25. a b c d

26. a b c d   27. a b c d   28. a b c d   29. a b c d   30. a b c d

31. a b c d   32. a b c d   33. a b c d   34. a b c d   35. a b c d

36. a b c d   37. a b c d   38. a b c d

Solutions with Explanation

LEVEL – 1

1. (b) Helicopter
2. (a) Cricket
3. (b) Rainbow
4. (d) Climber. Climbers are plants that take the support of something as their stems are weak and cannot stand on their own.
5. (b) Basketball. A game played by two teams.
6. (b)   7. (c)
8. (b)   9. (c)
10. (b)
11. (a) Christmas – Name of a festival.
12. (c) hill
13. (b) Box
14. (c) 'some' as sugar is uncountable.
15. (b) Stories.
16. (b) Uncle
17. (a) Computer – It is neither male nor female.
18. (c) Sania Mirza
19. (b)
20. (d) Kennel
21. (c) Library
22. (b) Plastic
23. (d) Calf
24. (c) Powder
25. (a) Terrific is not a noun.
26. (d)

LEVEL – 2

1. (d) children.
2. (a) sweaters
3. (c) slippers
4. (b) children
5. (a) Because they protect us from falling sick.
6. (c) My mother gave me a bouquet of flowers.
7. (b) Has someone seen a pride of lions?
8. (c) Go left, and then you will see a flight of steps.
9. (b) We saw a shoal of fish swimming in shallow water. A group of fish is called a shoal or a school.
10. (c) There was a troop of monkeys swinging on the trees. Litter is a group of dogs or cats.
11. (d) sand   12. (c) money

13.	**(a)**	grass	**14.**	**(d)**	hair
15.	**(b)**	thieves	**16.**	**(a)**	wolves
17.	**(b)**	knives	**18.**	**(b)**	monkeys

19. **(a)** babies
20. **(a)** Ram
21. **(c)** Tinkle
22. **(b)** America is a proper noun
23. **(b)** Rekha is a proper noun.
24. **(c)** January is a proper noun.
25. **(c)** Tia is the name of a person.
26. **(d)** medal is a thing; others refer to people.
27. **(d)** thumb
28. **(b)** Feminine 'Mare' is an adult female horse.
29. **(b)** uniform
30. **(b)** april, march june, july, august. There are twelve months in a year. They are January, February, March, April, May, June, July, August, September, October, November, December. One year has 365 days except for a leap year that comes after every four years. A leap year has 366 days.
31. **(c)** sweets
32. **(d)** churches
33. **(d)** schools
34. **(d)** shelves
35. **(c)** Eel
36. **(d)** Lounge
37. **(d)** Salad
38. **(b)** Baby deer is called a fawn.

2 CHAPTER FOREWORD

In this chapter, you will learn about words which are used in place of naming words. Such words are called pronouns.

Here is an activity for you which is based on pronouns.

Directions: Read the following story carefully and fill in the blanks with suitable pronouns in the blank spaces.

There was a beautiful princess called Melinda. She lived with ________________ father and mother in a huge palace. Everyone loved ________________. ________________ was good to one and all. Unfortunately, one day ________________ fell very sick. The doctors tried to cure ________________. But ________________ could not be saved! She was a beautiful princess!

Chapter 2

Pronouns

LEARNING OBJECTIVES

This lesson will help you to

- understand pronouns.
- use pronouns in place of nouns.
- make better sentences.

INTRODUCTION

We all know that pronouns are words that are used in place of naming words.

For example: I, She, He, You, are used for one person. We, They, and You are used for more than one person. It is used for animals, places and things.

There are :

It is a chair.   He is a boy.   She is a girl.

Possessive pronouns: Words used in place of nouns to show that something belongs to someone are called possessive pronouns. Yours, mine, theirs, hers and his are possessive pronouns.

This car is mine.   This is our car.

Objective pronouns: Words like me, us, them, whom her, him, it, and you are the object of the sentence.
For example: Mr. Paul will buy a car for him.

Demonstrative pronouns : Words such as this, that, these and those are called demonstrative pronouns.

- **This** is used when we want to tell of a single thing near us.

- **That** is used when we want to tell about a single thing not near to us.

- **These** is used to tell about more than one thing near to us.

- **Those** is used to tell about more than one thing not near to us.

Remember

❖ Objective pronouns are the object and not the subject of the sentence.

This is a cow.

That is a calf.

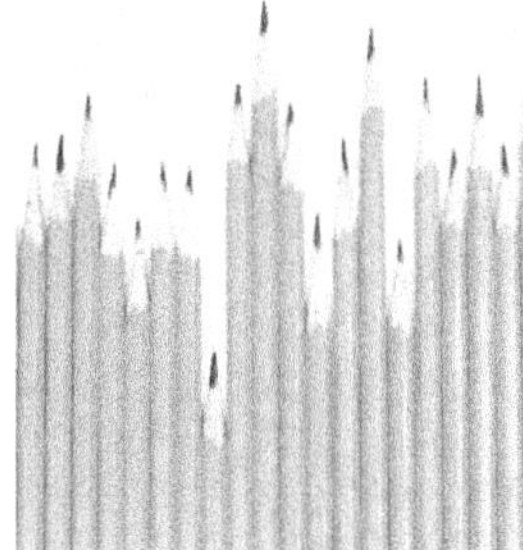

These are pencils.

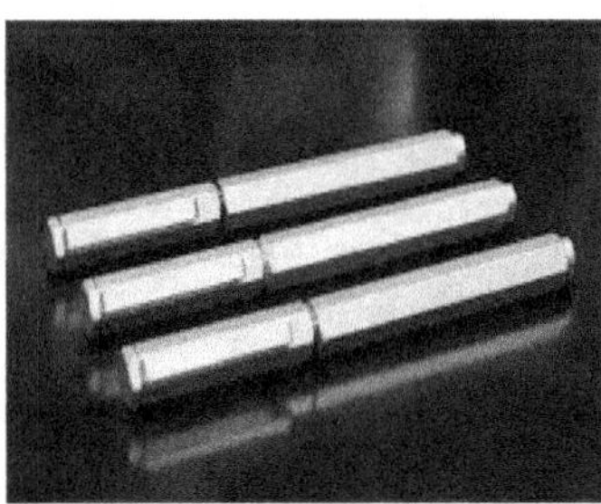

Those are pens.

Multiple Choice Questions

LEVEL – 1

Directions (Qs. 1-15): Read the sentences and choose the correct answer from the options given below.

1. Neha and Sneha are sisters. _______ live near that building.

    (a) He   (b) They   (c) She   (d) We

2. Ramya sings well. _______ has been taking classes.   [2015]

    (a) He   (b) She   (c) We   (d) They

3. Get ready quickly, Sam. _______ are getting late for school.

    (a) He   (b) She   (c) We   (d) They

4. Mr. Forge is a postman. _______ gets letters every day.

    (a) He   (b) She   (c) We   (d) They

5. Sameera and I dance well. _______ love dancing.   [2014]

    (a) He   (b) She   (c) They   (d) We

6. Ryan ran very fast. _______ won the first prize.

    (a) He   (b) She   (c) We   (d) They

7. My mother is a good cook. _______ cooks tasty food   [2016]

    (a) He   (b) She   (c) They   (d) We

8. Srishti writes well. _______ writes for the school magazines.

    (a) He   (b) She   (c) We   (d) They

9. My father goes to office every day. _______ goes by car.

    (a) He   (b) She   (c) We   (d) They

10. My trousers are old. I have worn _______ for a long time.   [2017]

    (a) him   (b) them   (c) her   (d) it

11. Look at Sam and Bob. What are _______ doing?

    (a) he   (b) she   (c) we   (d) they

12. Don't be such a bully! These are _______ . So I shall play with them.

    (a) mine   (b) yours   (c) his   (d) hers

13. Come and join _______,we are sowing seeds.

    (a) us   (b) we   (c) me   (d) your

14. They are John and Ana. That house belongs to ______

    (a) them (b) us (c) we (d) they

15. That is your book. This book is ______ .

    (a) mine (b) yours (c) ours (d) theirs

Directions (Qs. 16–20): Read the sentences carefully and fill in the blanks from the options given below.

16. Mom said to Arushi" Hurry up, Arushi! ______ are getting late for ______ school.

    (a) you, your (b) your, you (c) we, you (d) my, i

17. ______ is a big house. ______ all stay there happily. [2013]

    (a) He, his (b) Ours, we (c) You, yours (d) My, mine

18. ______, bought our shoes, they bought ______.

    (a) We, ours (b) We, theirs (c) They, them (d) I, they

19. ______ want to present this piano to you. Now it is ______.

    (a) He, you (b) I, yours (c) They, theirs (d) We, ours

20. Dad Scolded Ravi "Give Them Back ______ ball. It is not ______ .

    (a) their, yours (b) his her (c) we, ours (d) her, us

Directions (Qs. 21-25) : Fill in the blanks with correct option.

21. _________ is a teacher.

    (a) He (b) It (c) She (d) Them

22. _________ are playing in the park.

    (a) He (b) Us (c) They (d) Him

23. ____________ is my cycle.

    (a) I   (b) You   (c) Her   (d) It

24. ____________ are our new neighbours.

    (a) They   (b) Them   (c) Us   (d) We

25. We share ____________ lunch.

    (a) you   (b) our   (c) her   (d) them

26. This is where __________ met your sister.   [2018]

    (a) mine   (b) my   (c) me   (d) I

27. I can't find ________ new shirt anywhere.   [2019]

    (a) you   (b) I   (c) my   (d) we

28. ________ looks very sore. Did you hurt yourself ?   [2019]

    (a) Those   (b) These   (c) That   (d) Them

29. Let ________ help you carry these books.   [2021]
    (a) I   (b) me
    (c) my   (d) you

30. Rashika is a brilliant student. ________ always comes first in her class.
                                                                          [2022]

    (a) He   (b) Her
    (c) She   (d) Him

31. The Statue of Unity is a monument. __________ is located in Gujarat. [2022]

A. He
B. She
C. It
D. None of these

LEVEL – 2

Directions (Qs. 1–10): Read the passage and fill in the blanks with the correct pronouns from the options given below.   **[Tricky]**

(1) ____ am Arjun and (2) ______ is my friend Manish. (3) ______ are neighbours and (4) ____ go to school in the school bus everyday. (5)______ is a big yellow and green bus. Have (6) ______ ever travelled in a bus? (7) _______ is very exciting. Many people ride in buses. (8) ______ use them to reach their offices. That is Akshat. (9) ______ has a car that drops him to school every day. When (10) ______ grow I want to become a bus driver and Manish could be a conductor.

1.	(a)	He	(b)	She	(c)	I	(d) We
2.	(a)	he	(b)	she	(c)	i	(d) we
3.	(a)	He	(b)	She	(c)	We	(d) They
4.	(a)	he	(b)	she	(c)	we	(d) they
5.	(a)	He	(b)	She	(c)	It	(d) We
6.	(a)	he	(b)	she	(c)	they	(d) you
7.	(a)	It	(b)	He	(c)	We	(d) They
8.	(a)	They	(b)	He	(c)	She	(d) It
9.	(a)	He	(b)	She	(c)	They	(d) It
10.	(a)	he	(b)	she	(c)	I	(d) they

Directions (Qs. 11–14): Fill in the blanks with a correct pronoun. Choose the answers from the options given below.

11. I will go to a movie with ______.

(a) they
(b) them
(c) us
(d) we

12. You do not speak to ______, she is very rude.

   (a) him   (b) her   (c) you   (d) I

13. The visitors danced with ______.

   (a) us   (b) we   (c) they   (d) I

14. Kelly is buying a doll for ______

   (a) her   (b) she   (c) they   (d) we

Directions (Qs. 15–18): Read the passage given below and replace the underlined words with the pronouns from the options given below.

(15) <u>Sameer and I</u> were very excited about going for an outing to the rail museum. I love to know different types of transport, train is one of them. Sameer is also interested in knowing about different types of vehicles. (16) <u>Sameer</u> has already visited so many museums. (17) <u>Sameer and his parents always</u> go to different museums for outings. This is my first outing to a museum. I will go to a museum for the first time (18). <u>Sameer and I</u> will go by his car.

15. (a) We   (b) They   (c) Us   (d) Our

16. (a) He   (b) She   (c) We   (d) You

17. (a) Them   (b) They   (c) We   (d) Us

18. (a) He   (b) My   (c) She   (d) We

19. Which of the following moves on land ?

(a)   (b)   (c)   (d)

Directions (Qs. 20–23): Replace the underlined nouns with pronouns. Choose the answers from the options given below.

20. Mr. Smith has a black fur coat. <u>**The coat**</u> is made of real fur.

   (a) It   (b) She   (c) We   (d) They

21. <u>Saima</u> went to the park yesterday.

   (a) He   (b) She   (c) We   (d) It

22. <u>Sam, Sameer and George</u> have gone to buy vegetables

   (a) He   (b) They   (c) She   (d) Them

23. <u>Veena, Seema and Salma</u> will go in their car.

    (a) They   (b) We   (c) He   (d) She

24. **In the grid given below how many pronouns can you find? [Critical Thinking]**

h	t	u	n	h	k	y	e	a	y
p	t	n	h	v	o	t	f	h	u
e	y	h	e	r	p	p	r	e	r
m	h	g	h	k	i	o	e	f	k
h	i	m	n	m	y	s	e	l	f
f	t	i	m	e	i	h	j	h	j
s	j	n	m	f	i	e	n	l	l
h	u	e	k	g	j	k	m	m	g

    (a) 8   (b) 6   (c) 3   (d) 4

Directions (Qs. 25–28): Look at the picture and choose the correct sentence.

25. (a) She is writing with a pen.   (b) He is writing with a pencil.

    (c) We are writing with a pen.   (d) They are writing with a pen.

26. (a) He is a tigers mask.   (b) She is a tiger mask.

    (c) It is a tiger mask.   (d) We are a tiger mask.

27. (a) He is a clock.   (b) She is a clock.

(c) It is a clock.   (d) We are a clock.

28. (a) She fell from the tree.   (b) It fell from the tree

(c) He fell from the tree.   (d) They fell on the tree.

29. Please give your notebook to ___________.   **(2020)**

(a) I   (b) mine

(c) our   (d) me

30. A lot of volunteers are offering ___________ help.   **(2020)**

(a) they   (b) their

(c) there   (d) hers

RESPONSE GRID

LEVEL 1

1. a b c d	2. a b c d	3. a b c d	4. a b c d	5. a b c d
6. a b c d	7. a b c d	8. a b c d	9. a b c d	10. a b c d
11. a b c d	12. a b c d	13. a b c d	14. a b c d	15. a b c d
16. a b c d	17. a b c d	18. a b c d	19. a b c d	20. a b c d
21. a b c d	22. a b c d	23. a b c d	24. a b c d	25. a b c d
26. a b c d	27. a b c d	28. a b c d	29. a b c d	30. a b c d
31. a b c d				

LEVEL 2

1. a b c d	2. a b c d	3. a b c d	4. a b c d	5. a b c d
6. a b c d	7. a b c d	8. a b c d	9. a b c d	10. a b c d
11. a b c d	12. a b c d	13. a b c d	14. a b c d	15. a b c d
16. a b c d	17. a b c d	18. a b c d	19. a b c d	20. a b c d
21. a b c d	22. a b c d	23. a b c d	24. a b c d	25. a b c d
26. a b c d	27. a b c d	28. a b c d	29. a b c d	30. a b c d

Solutions with Explanations

LEVEL – 1

1. **(b)** Neha and Sneha are sisters. They live near that building.
2. **(b)** Ramya sings well. She has been taking classes.
3. **(c)** Get ready quickly, Sam. We are getting late for school.
4. **(a)** Mr. Forge is a postman. He gets letters every day.
5. **(d)** Sameera and I dance well. We love dancing.
6. **(a)** Ryan ran very fast. He won the first prize.
7. **(b)** My mother is a good cook. She cooks tasty food.
8. **(b)** Srishti writes well. She writes for the school magazines.
9. **(a)** My father goes to office every day. He goes by car.
10. **(b)** My trousers are old. I have worn them for a long time.
11. **(d)** Look at Sam and Bob. What are they doing?
12. **(a)** Don't be such a bully! These are mine. So I shall play with them.
13. **(a)** Come and join us, we are sowing seeds.
14. **(a)** They are John and Ana. That house belongs to them.
15. **(a)** That is your book. This book is mine.
16. **(a)** Mom said to Arushi" Hurry up, Arushi! You are getting late for your school.
17. **(b)** Ours is a big house. We all stay there happily.
18. **(b)** We bought our shoes, they bought theirs.
19. **(b)** I want to present this piano to you. Now it is yours.
20. **(a)** Dad Scolded Ravi " Give Them Back their ball. It is not yours".
21. **(a)** He
22. **(c)** They
23. **(d)** It
24. **(a)** They
25. **(b)** our
26. **(d)** I
27. **(c)** my
28. **(c)** That
29. **(b)** Let me help you carry your books.

30. **(c)** In this black adverb must be used, so she will come in the blank.
31. **(c)**

LEVEL – 2

1. **(c)** I
2. **(a)** he
3. **(c)** We
4. **(c)** we
5. **(c)** It
6. **(d)** you
7. **(a)** It
8. **(a)** They
9. **(a)** He
10. **(c)** I
11. **(a)** Mr. Smith wants to give the gift to you.
12. **(b)** I will go to a movie with them.
13. **(b)** You do not speak to her, she is very rude.
14. **(a)** The visitors danced with us.
15. **(a)** Kelly is buying a doll for her.
16. **(a)** We   17. **(a)** He
18. **(b)** They   18. **(d)** We
19. **(d)** Car
20. **(a)** Mr. Smith has a black fur coat. It is made of real fur.
21. **(b)** She went to the park yesterday.
22. **(b)** They have gone to buy vegetables.
23. **(a)** They will go in their car.
24. **(a)** him, her, mine, myself, she, me, I, he
25. **(b)** He is writing with a pen.
26. **(c)** It is a tiger mask.
27. **(c)** It is a clock.
28. **(b)** A fruit is falling from a tree. We use the pronoun 'it' to refer to animals or things.
29. **(d)** me
30. **(b)** their

In this chapter, you will learn about action words. These words are called verbs. Action words show what action is going on or being talked about in the sentence. Here is an exercise for you based on verbs.

Directions: Complete the story given below by filling the blanks. Choose the best option.

Harikesh was having a bath in the pond near his house. His sister Netra was (1) ________________ near the pond with a towel in her hand. Harikesh was enjoying himself. He (2) ________________ the whole length of the pool again and again. Suddenly there was a loud (3) ________________. Netra (4) ________________ around. Harikesh had (5) ________________. Netra started (6) ________________ for help. A passerby quickly jumped into the pond. He (7) ________________ deep into the pond. He found Harikesh lying senseless near a broken boat. He (8) ________________ him up. Harikesh was hurt. They (9) ________________ him to the nearby clinic. He was (10) ________________ in an hour's time. Everyone was happy.

1. (i) standing   (ii) crying   (iii) crawling
2. (i) walked   (ii) swam   (iii) ran
3. (i) jump   (ii) knock   (iii) crash
4. (i) stood   (ii) looked   (iii) heard
5. (i) disappeared   (ii) walked   (iii) run
6. (i) crying   (ii) shouting   (iii) jumping
7. (i) jumped   (ii) dived   (iii) pushed
8. (i) waved   (ii) hurried   (iii) pulled
9. (i) pull   (ii) push   (iii) took
10. (i) woken   (ii) cured   (iii) given

Verbs

> Remember
>
> ❖ Every sentence has a verb.
> ❖ Verb says something about the subject.
>
> **For example:**
>
> The dog <u>chased</u> the cat.
>
> The dog ⇒ Subject
>
> Chased ⇒ Verb

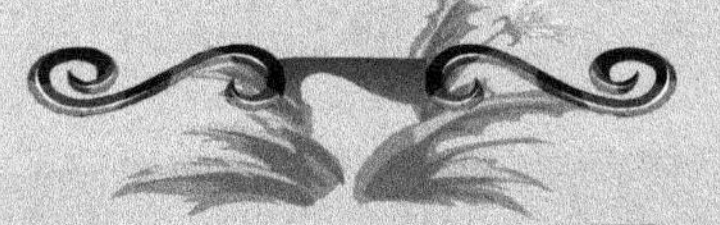

LEARNING OBJECTIVE

This lesson will help you to

- learn what are verbs.
- recognise different types of verbs.
- understand how to use verbs in making sentences.

DEFINITION

The words that tell us about actions or words that show that some work is being done are called action words, doing words or Verbs. Dance, paint, smile or read, they all show that some action is being done. Verbs are an important part of a sentence.

Dance   Read   Paint

Smile   Laugh   Fall

INTRODUCTION

When you find yourself confused whether a sentence has an action word or not, look at all words in the given sentence and ask yourself "is this something that a person or an object can do"?

For example: A boy is reading a book.

Here the word reading is a verb or an action word. It suggests that an action is being done. If a verb is not used in a sentence the sentence seems to be incomplete.

For example: When I say "I will school".

> Does it have any meaning?
>
> Now let us add 'go' to it, and write it as
>
> "I will go to school".

We find that just by adding an action word to the whole sentence we are able to add meaning to a sentence.

There are two forms of verbs. **Doing words** and **Being Words.** Doing words are words that tell us about some action taking place.

For example: Jump, Pull.

A boy is **reading** a book

Jump   Pull

BEING VERBS

Being verbs do not denote any action or doing, but they link the subject to the verb. The most common linking verb is 'to be'.

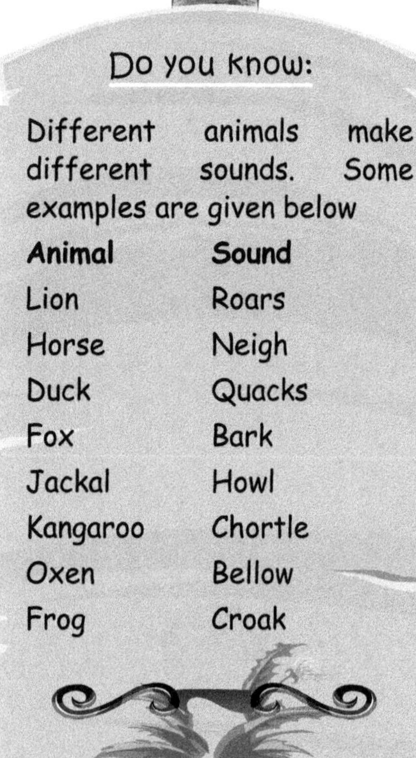

Do you know:

Different animals make different sounds. Some examples are given below

Animal	Sound
Lion	Roars
Horse	Neigh
Duck	Quacks
Fox	Bark
Jackal	Howl
Kangaroo	Chortle
Oxen	Bellow
Frog	Croak

To Be: The various forms of it being, am, is, are, were, was, be, being, been.

There are many rules to use being words.

We use 'am' with 'I'

We always use 'is' with 'he', 'she' and 'it'. (singular words)

'Are' is used with 'We', 'they' and 'you'. (Plural words)

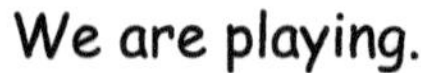

We are playing.

I am playing.

They are going.

He is going to school.

Multiple Choice Questions

LEVEL – 1

Directions (Qs. 1–10): Look at the following pictures and select the verb that describes the action in the picture. Choose the answers from the options given below

1. (a) Wash   (b) Talk   (c) Brush   (d) Cough

2. (a) Dance   (b) Sit   (c) Swim   (d) Sleep

3. (a) Snore   (b) Run   (c) Drink   (d) Stand

4. (a) Fight   (b) Read   (c) Eat   (d) Laugh

5. (a) write   (b) Climb   (c) Think   (d) Cook

6. (a) Pray   (b) Think   (c) Eat   (d) Wash

7. (a) Eat   (b) Wash   (c) Read   (d) Drink

8. (a) Crawl   (b) Walk   (c) Drink   (d) Eat

9. (a) Run   (b) Paint   (c) Walk   (d) Wash

10. (a) Sneeze   (b) Laugh   (c) Talk   (d) Eat

Directions (Qs. 11-13) : Fill in the blanks with right verb by choosing the correct option.

11. Ayesha __________ a smart girl.   **(2016)**

     (a) am   (b) is   (c) were   (d) are

12. I _____________ going to the market.
    (a) is   (b) are   (c) were   (d) am

13. Saina Nehwal _____________ a badminton player.   **(2015)**
    (a) we   (b) is   (c) am   (d) are

Directions (Qs. 14-18) : Look at the pictures and choose the correct option.
    (2014)

14. (a) The children are playing in the park.   (b) The children are reading books.

    (c) The children are sleeping.   (d) The children are playing at the beach.

15. (a) Patter cake, Patter cake.   (b) Bake me a cake.

    (c) The baker bakes a cake.   (d) Bakers man.

(2013)

16. (a) Rita goes jogging everyday.   (b) She is walking.

    (c) Children are playing.   (d) Rita is walking in the park.

17. (a) Cobbler, Cobbler mend my shoe.   (b) The cobbler mends our shoes.

    (c) The shoes are new.   (d) The socks are new.

18. (a) Lotus temple was built by Shah Jahan.

    (b) The Taj Mahal was built by Shah Jahan.

    (c) The Taj Mahal is a house.

    (d) My name is Akbar.

19. ___________ you ever eaten roast chicken ?   (2018)

    (a) Has   (b) Have   (c) Have had   (d) Having

Direction (Q. 20): Choose the correct answer.

Example

Which animal does not have legs?

    (a) Horse   (b) Fish   (c) Cat   (b) Dog

20. **Identify the word which is a verb.**   (2021)

    (a) General   (b) Satisfy   (c) Brutally   (d) Wisdom

21. **The stars are <u>twinkling</u> in the night sky.**   (2022)

    (a) Adverb   (b) Noun   (c) Verb   (d) Pronoun

22. **Arjun is ________ on the road.**   (2022)

    (a) walked   (b) walking   (c) walk   (d) walks

23. **She wore a ________ dress on her birthday.**   (2022)

    (a) beautiful   (b) more beautiful

    (c) beautifully   (d) morst beautiful

24. **The elephant ________ eating the bananas.**   (2022)

    (a) are   (b) is   (c) has   (d) have

25. There _______ many trees in the garden. (2022)

  (a) has   (b) have   (c) is   (d) are

LEVEL - 2

Directions (Qs. 1–10): Read the sentences given below and choose the correct one. [Critical Thinking]

1. (a) That worker is digging.   (b) His hands is dirty.
  (c) They love to playing football.   (d) I am ate food.

2. (a) John is walking on the road.   (b) Jay and Mary is eating.
  (c) Mom cooking food.   (d) I am cannot go.

3. (a) I go to Qutub Minar.   (b) Many people have love sports.
  (c) Krishna will eating food.   (d) My brother is watching television.

4. (a) That man vomiting   (b) I have read that book.
  (c) Many children playing the park.   (d) The car will stopping.

5. (a) The building was huge.   (b) I has heard the lions roar.
  (c) Leopard rans very fast.   (d) Dad given car keys to watchman.

6. (a) I am not going, you can go.   (b) They is all playing.
  (c) The dogs is barking.   (d) What are this?

7. (a) She are an obedient girl.
  (b) We are students of this school.
  (c) I is going to eat my dinner at 9o clock.
  (d) He are not playing football.

8. (a) We is an intelligent children, we know what is to be done.
  (b) They are all very well educated.
  (c) Last year, he was in India only.
  (d) This are my pictures, you can't take them away.

9. (a) Tom and Rim are playing chess.
  (b) Mr.Rogers are out of his house.
  (c) We is participating in the school play.
  (d) I is very hungry, I will have my food and then come.

10. (a) This year we is going to San Francisco for vacations.

    (b) They is going for a picnic tomorrow.

    (c) Today is a working day. We have to go to school.

    (d) He are talking to his friend.

Directions (Qs. 11–18): Read the passage given below and fill in the blanks with proper verbs choosing the answers from the options given below.

Once there was a boy. His name was Jay. He was a very naughty child. He loved to(11)___ pranks. One day, he (12)__________his father and (13)______ "Dad there's fire at home". His father left all his work and(14) ______ back home. To reach as early as he could, he (15)_______ his car very fast. He (16)_____ so fast that he lost control and his car(17) ___a truck. In the accident Jay's father lost both his legs. Jay was very sorry. He had (18)___ his lesson.

11. (a) eat   (b) play   (c) wash   (d) sneeze

12. (a) called   (b) promised   (c) wished   (d) washed

13. (a) cried   (b) laughed   (c) washed   (d) greeted

14. (a) crawled   (b) rushed   (c) sneezed   (d) eat

15. (a) walked   (b) drove   (c) washed   (d) liked

16. (a) drove   (b) washed   (c) painted   (d) cleaned

17. (a) fight   (b) hit   (c) cleaned   (d) scratched

18. (a) written   (b) learnt   (c) washed   (d) rowed

19. **Which of the following is true?**   **[Tricky]**

    (a) Jay was a naughty boy.   (b) Jay was a smart boy.

    (c) Jay went to school.   (d) Jay was climbing a tree.

Directions (Qs. 20–23): Read the following sentences and fill in the blanks from the options given below.

20. **What __________________?**

    (a) is she sitting   (b) are he eating   (c) is he going   (d) is he writing

21. **Where ___________?**

    (a) is they going   (b) did you go

    (c) are she reading   (d) do stay

22.**How _______?**

    (a) is you going   (b) did he write that letter

    (c) she are walking   (d) I is eating

23. Why _______________?

    (a)   has you not finished your work   (b)   is he not listening

    (c)   I are not going to the party   (d)   they is not eating their food

Directions (Qs. 24–25): Match the following animals with the sounds they make. Choose the answers from the options given below

24. A Duck_______.

    (a) runs   (b) quacks   (c) neighs   (d) jumps

25. A lion ________.

    (a) barks   (b) roars   (c) talks   (d) flops

26. A horse _______.

    (a) barks   (b) neighs   (c) oinks   (d) bleets

27. Jackals _________.

    (a) howl   (b) cluck   (c) bleat   (d) grunt

28. Kangaroo _______.

    (a) groan   (b) chortle   (c) chatter   (d) screech

29. Foxes _________.

    (a) croak   (b) bleat   (c) bellow   (d) bark

30. Oxen _______.

    (a) pipe   (b) croak   (c) bellow   (d) sing

31. I have always ________ that song was great.   **(2019)**

    (a) thinking   (b) think   (c) thought   (d) thinks

32. I really ________ to finish this work before 6 pm.   **(2020)**

    (a) has

    (b) have

    (c) was

    (d) having

> **Example**
>
> Sarah is riding ______ new bike.
> (a) she   (b) her
> (c) hers   (d) him

33. It was so ________ of us not to speak to each other.   **(2020)**

    (a) angry   (b) foolish   (c) anxious   (d) lazy

Directions (Qs. 34-36): Choose the most suitable option to complete each conversation.

Example

Jay: Can I come and play with you tomorrow?

Anita: Yeah, _________.

(a) Please do   (b) I want

(c) Let's go   (d) Up standing

34. Seema: Why don't you _______ the teacher?
Rati: Yes, you are right. Let me. (2021)
(a) asking   (b) asked   (c) ask   (d) asks

35. In order to _______ the order, press the red button. (2021)
(a) selected   (b) used   (c) place   (d) got

36. The Antarctic blue whale is the _______ mammal found on the earth.
(2022)
(a) largest   (b) large   (c) larger   (d) largely

RESPONSE GRID

LEVEL 1

1. a b c d   2. a b c d   3. a b c d   4. a b c d   5. a b c d
6. a b c d   7. a b c d   8. a b c d   9. a b c d   10. a b c d
11. a b c d   12. a b c d   13. a b c d   14. a b c d   15. a b c d
16. a b c d   17. a b c d   18. a b c d   19. a b c d   20. a b c d
21. a b c d   22. a b c d   23. a b c d   24. a b c d   25. a b c d

LEVEL 2

1. a b c d   2. a b c d   3. a b c d   4. a b c d   5. a b c d
6. a b c d   7. a b c d   8. a b c d   9. a b c d   10. a b c d
11. a b c d   12. a b c d   13. a b c d   14. a b c d   15. a b c d
16. a b c d   17. a b c d   18. a b c d   19. a b c d   20. a b c d
21. a b c d   22. a b c d   23. a b c d   24. a b c d   25. a b c d
26. a b c d   27. a b c d   28. a b c d   29. a b c d   30. a b c d
31. a b c d   32. a b c d   33. a b c d   34. a b c d   35. a b c d
36. a b c d

Solutions with Explanation

LEVEL - 1

1. (b) Talk		2. (a) Dance	
3. (c) Drink		4. (b) Read	
5. (c) Think		6. (a) Pray	
7. (a) Eat		8. (a) Crawl	
9. (b) Paint		10. (a) Sneeze	
11. (b) is		12. (d) am	
13. (b) is			

14. (d) The children are playing at the beach.

15. (c) The baker bakes a cake.

16. (a) Rita goes jogging everyday.

17. (b) The cobbler mends our shoes.

18. (b) The Taj Mahal was built by shah jahan.

19. (b) Have

20. (b) A verb is an action, so satisfy is a verb.

21. (c) Twinkling is an action and any action is a Verb.

22. (b) The sentence is in present continuous tense; hence, Verb+ ing must be used.

23. (a) She wore a beautiful dress on her birthday.

24. (b)   25.   (d)

LEVEL - 2

1. (a) That worker is digging.

2. (a) John is walking on the road.

3. (d) My brother is watching television.

4. (b) I have read that book.

5. (a) The building was huge.

6. (a) I am not going, you can go.

7. **(b)** We are students of this school.

8. **(b)** They are all very well educated.

9. **(a)** Tom and Rim are playing chess.

10. **(c)** Today is a working day. We have to go to school.

11. **(b)** play

12. **(a)** called

13. **(a)** cried

14. **(b)** rushed

15. **(b)** drove

16. **(a)** drove

17. **(b)** hit

18. **(b)** learnt

19. **(a)** Jay was a naughty boy.

20. **(d)** What is he writing?

21. **(b)** Where did you go?

22. **(b)** How did he write that letter?

23. **(b)** Why is he not listening?

24. **(b)** A duck quacks.

25. **(b)** A lion roars.

26. **(b)** A horse neighs.

27. **(a)** Jackals howl. Chickens cluck. Goats bleat. Camels grunt.

28. **(b)** A Kangaroo chortles. Bears groan. Magpie chatters. Bats screech.

29. **(d)** Foxes bark, seals also bark. Frogs croak. Calves bleat. Koalas and oxen bellow.

30. **(c)** Oxen bellows

31. **(c)** thought

32. **(b)** have

33. **(b)** foolish

34. **(c)** Why don't you ask the teacher?

35. **(c)** In order to place the order, press the red button.

36. **(a)** The Antarctic whale is the largest mammal found on the earth.

 # CHAPTER FOREWORD

In this chapter, you will learn about words which tell about 'time' of action in a sentence. These words are called tenses. Tenses tell the reader wether an action has already taken place or is going on or will take place in the future.

Here is an exercise for you.

Directions : Look at the pictures. Write a sentence for each of them in the present tense.

1. _______________________________________

2. _______________________________________

3. _______________________________________

4. _______________________________________

5. _______________________________________

4
Chapter

Tenses

INTRODUCTION

- Tenses are also known as yesterday, today and tomorrow words. They tell us whether something has already happened or is happening or is about to happen.
- In simple present tense if only one person is talked about, we use singular verbs.

For example:

A boy **runs.**   A girl **reads.**

- If more than one person is being talked about, we use plural verbs.

For example:

We **run.**   We **read.**

Remember

❖ We use present simple tense to talk about things we know to be true.

- The action that is taking place now is said to be in present tense i.e today.

For example:

I **play** chess with my friends.

The word **play** tell us that the action is **taking place**.

- We also use present tense to tell **about actions that are habits**, or **tell about things** that **are true**.

For example:

I **go** to school daily.   The Sun **rises** in the East.

- Words that tell us about actions that are still happening are called to be in present tense.

For example : My mother is washing clothes

The word **washing** tell us that an action is regular.

- The action that happened in the past is said to be in past tense i.e. yesterday

For example: I worked hard.

The word **worked** tell us that the action was in past tense.

- The action that is about to take place is said to be in the future i.e. tomorrow.

For example: My mother **will wash** clothes.

I **will play** chess.

The words 'will wash' and 'will play' are tomorrow words or future tense words.

Here we will deal only with **Simple present tense.**

My mother is **washing** clothes.

Multiple Choice Questions

LEVEL - 1

Directions (Qs. 1-10): Read the following sentences and fill in the blanks with the correct simple present tenses. Choose answers from the options given below

1. Kunal ___ very fast. He won the first prize in racing.

   (a) runs (b) running (c) run (d) ran

2. I ___ school at 7 o' clock every day.

   (a) goes to (b) go to (c) going to (d) go

3. He ______ the poem so well that he always wins in the competition.

   (a) recited (b) recite (c) recites (d) reciting

4. He ______ to collect stamps.

   (a) likes (b) liked (c) like (d) liking

5. My mother is a great cook, she___ good food.

   (a) cooked (b) cook (c) cooks (d) cooking

6. He ___ up early in the morning daily.

   (a) get (b) got (c) getting (d) gets

7. The President of India ___ in the Rashtrapati Bhawan.

   (a) lives (b) live (c) living (d) lived

8. He ______ very good Spanish.

   (a) spoken (b) spoke (c) speaking (d) speaks

9. Shreyas _________ to eat ice cream even during winters.

   (a) like (b) liked (c) liking (d) likes

10. He ____ cricket in the park.

    (a) plays (b) played (c) playing (d) play

Directions (Qs. 11–15) : Answer the following questions with the correct use of tense.

11. Does he study daily? (2015)

Yes; he __________ daily.

(a) study   (b) will study   (c) studies   (d) studied

12. What time is the next train?

The next train ______ at 8.00 pm.

(a) was   (b) are   (c) is   (d) were

13. Where are you going during summer holidays? (2017)

I ______ to Shimla during summer holidays.

(a) is going   (b) was going   (c) am going   (d) will be going

14. How did you spend your holiday? (2014)

I ______ my holiday playing and eating.

(a) spend   (b) spends   (c) spent   (d) was spent

15. What time does he sleep at night? (2016)

He ______ at 9.00 pm every night.

(a) is sleeping   (b) sleeps   (c) slept   (d) will sleep

Directions (Qs. 16-20) : Complete the sentences and fill in the crossword.

16. The birds __________ to far away countries in winter. (2016)

(a) fly   (b) flew   (c) flown   (d) flies

17. The girls always __________ to classical music.

(a) listening   (b) listens   (c) listen   (d) all of these

18. Chris never _________ jeans.   **(2013)**

    (a) wear   (b) wears   (c) wearing   (d) none of these

19. We sometimes _________ books.

    (a) read   (b) reading   (c) reads   (d) none of these

20. She _________ like to drink milk every day.   **(2017)**

    (a) doesn't   (b) don't   (c) dont   (d) do

21. I _________ my work.   **(2019)**

    (a) am doing   (b) are doing   (c) is doing   (d) was do

22. Rohan asked his mother to _______ him science.   **(2021)**
    (a) study   (b) teach
    (c) learn   (d) understand

23. Seema didn't ______ the idea of picnic.   **(2021)**
    (a) liked   (b) liking
    (c) like   (d) likes

LEVEL – 2

Directions (Qs. 1–15): Read the passage carefully and fill in the blanks with simple present tense words. Choose the answers from the options given below.

I always __(1) to drive cars. Wake me up any time and you will find me ready to go for a drive. I __(2) up very early in the morning, quickly __(3) my teeth and __(4) ready to drive my car. I __(5) for a long drive for about an hour. After coming back I __(6) ready within half an hour and __(7) for work. I __(8) my car from my house to office. After reaching office I __(9) and sit on my seat. Everyone in my office __(10) before 9'o clock otherwise they get absent marked. There is a fixed seat for everyone who is __(11) in my office. After I __(12) office I start doing the work that has been planned for that day. I have a few friends in my office. We all __(13) for outings. We __(14) and __(15)for picnics.

1.   (a) love   (b) loves   (c) loved   (d) loving

2.   (a) get   (b) gets   (c) getting   (d) go

3.   (a) brushed   (b) brushing   (c) brushes   (d) brush

4.   (a) get   (b) getting   (c) got   (d) gets

5.   (a) go   (b) goes   (c) going   (d) gone

6. (a) gets   (b) get   (c) getting   (d) got

7. (a) leaves   (b) leave   (c) leaving   (d) left

8. (a) driving   (b) drives   (c) driving   (d) drive

9. (a) gone   (b) goes   (c) go   (d) going

10. (a) reaching   (b) reaches   (c) reach   (d) reached

11. (a) works   (b) work   (c) working   (d) worked

12. (a) reach   (b) reaching   (c) reached   (d) reaches

13. (a) goes   (b) go   (c) going   (d) gone

14. (a) drive   (b) drove   (c) drives   (d) driving

15. (a) go   (b) goes   (c) going   (d) gone

Directions (Qs. 16–25): Read the following sentences and recognise the simple tense words. Choose the answers from the options given below.

16. **I always go to school on time.**

     (a) I   (b) go   (c) school   (d) time.

17. **Normally do you sleep late at night?**

     (a) do   (b) you   (c) sleep   (d) late

18. **Does he take tuitions for Maths?**

     (a) take   (b) he   (c) tuitions   (d) for

19. **Does Mr. Ashok teach in that school?**

     (a) Does   (b) teach   (c) in   (d) that

20. **I am Siddhant I study in Fifth class.**

     (a) I   (b) am   (c) study   (d) fifth

21. **I am sure that he knows the answer.**

     (a) I   (b) sure   (c) knows   (d) answer

22. **Sam goes to the nearby library.**

     (a) Sam   (b) goes   (c) to   (d) the

23. **Mrs. Jannet runs a parlour.**

     (a) runs   (b) a   (c) parlour   (d) Mrs Jannet

24. He practices for the upcoming race every day.

    (a) practices   (b) upcoming   (c) race   (d) every day

25. He writes amazing stories.

    (a) He   (b) writes   (c) amazing   (d) stories

Directions (Qs. 26–30): Read the following riddles and fill in the blanks. Choose the answers from the options given below.

I ____you up everyday

I start your day

You can't look at me

But I give you light to see everywhere.

26. (a) wake   (b) woke   (c) waked   (d) waking

I am the

National bird of India

With beautiful feathers

I love to spread them

And______in the rains.

27. (a) dances   (b) dance   (c) danced   (d) dancing

I am a starfish

I _____in water

28. (a) swims   (b) swimming   (c) swim   (d) swam

I am a lotus

National flower of India.

I _____in muddy water.

29. (a) bloomed   (b) blooming   (c) blooms   (d) bloom

I am a tiger

I live in a group

I _____to run very fast.

30. (a) loves   (b) loved   (c) love   (d) loving

31. It is only 2 p.m. and the train __________ until 4 p.m. today.   (2018)

    (a) goes   (b) isn't going   (c) hasn't gone   (d) gone

32. Raina: _______ did Jiya learn ballet?   (2021)

    (a) What   (b) Whom

    (c) When   (d) Who

RESPONSE GRID

LEVEL 1

1. a b c d   2. a b c d   3. a b c d   4. a b c d   5. a b c d

6. a b c d   7. a b c d   8. a b c d   9. a b c d   10. a b c d

11. a b c d   12. a b c d   13. a b c d   14. a b c d   15. a b c d

16. a b c d   17. a b c d   18. a b c d   19. a b c d   20. a b c d

21. a b c d   22. a b c d   23. a b c d

LEVEL 2

1. a b c d   2. a b c d   3. a b c d   4. a b c d   5. a b c d

6. a b c d   7. a b c d   8. a b c d   9. a b c d   10. a b c d

11. a b c d   12. a b c d   13. a b c d   14. a b c d   15. a b c d

16. a b c d   17. a b c d   18. a b c d   19. a b c d   20. a b c d

21. a b c d   22. a b c d   23. a b c d   24. a b c d   25. a b c d

26. a b c d   27. a b c d   28. a b c d   29. a b c d   30. a b c d

31. a b c d   32. a b c d

Solutions with Explanation

LEVEL – 1

1. **(a)** Kunal runs very fast. He won first prize in racing.

2. **(b)** I go to school at 7 o clock every day.

3. **(c)** He recites the poem so well that he always wins in the competition.

4. **(a)** He likes to collect stamps.

5.   **(c)**   My mother is a great cook, she cooks good food.

6.   **(d)**   He gets up early in the morning.

7.   **(a)**   The President of India lives in the Rashtrapati Bhawan.

8.   **(d)**   He speaks very good Spanish.

9.   **(d)**   Shreyas likes to eat ice cream even during winters.

10.   **(a)**   He plays cricket in the park.

11.	**(c)** studies		12.	**(c)** is
13.	**(c)** an going		14.	**(c)** spent
15.	**(b)** sleeps		16.	**(a)** fly
17.	**(c)** listen		18.	**(b)** wears
19.	**(a)** read		20.	**(a)** doesn't

21. **(a)** am doing

22. **(b)** Rohan asked his mother to teach him science.

23. **(c)** Seema didn't like the idea of Picnic.

LEVEL – 2

1.	**(a)** love		2.	**(a)** get
3.	**(d)** brush		4.	**(a)** get
5.	**(a)** go		6.	**(b)** get
7.	**(b)** leave		8.	**(d)** drive
9.	**(c)** go		10.	**(b)** reaches
11.	**(c)** working		12.	**(a)** reach
13.	**(b)** go		14.	**(a)** drive
15.	**(a)** go		16.	**(b)** go
17.	**(c)** sleep		18.	**(a)** take
19.	**(b)** teach		20.	**(c)** study
21.	**(c)** knows		22.	**(b)** goes
23.	**(a)** runs		24.	**(a)** practices
25.	**(b)** writes		26.	**(a)** wake
27.	**(b)** dance		28.	**(c)** swim
29.	**(d)** bloom		30.	**(c)** love

31. **(b)** isn't going

32. **(c)** When did Jiya learnt ballet?

<table><tr><td>**5**</td><td></td></tr></table>

CHAPTER FOREWORD

In this chapter, you will learn about describing words. These describing words, known as adjectives, tell us something more about the things we are talking about in the sentence.

Here is an exercise for you which you will enjoy doing.

Directions: This is the picture of a dog called Fluffy. Using words from the box write 5 lines about Fluffy.

White,   Ribbon,   Brown eyes,   Curly tail,   Black spots.

1. ____

____

2. ____

____

3. ____

____

4. ____

____

5. ____

5
Chapter

Adjectives

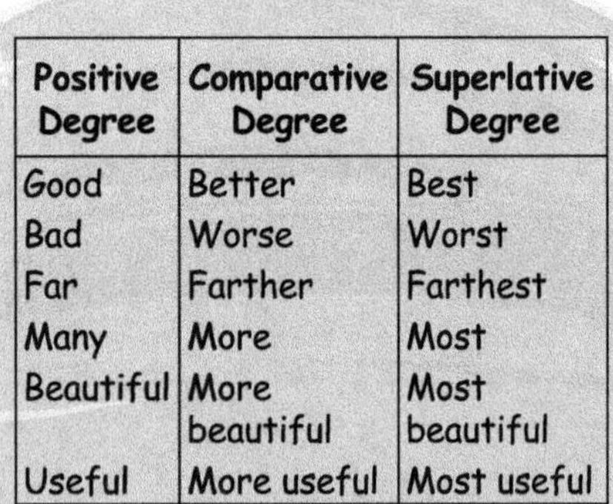

Positive Degree	Comparative Degree	Superlative Degree
Good	Better	Best
Bad	Worse	Worst
Far	Farther	Farthest
Many	More	Most
Beautiful	More beautiful	Most beautiful
Useful	More useful	Most useful

LEARNING OBJECTIVES

This lesson will help you to
- learn describing words
- use adjectives for nouns and pronouns

DEFINITION

Adjectives are describing words. They help in knowing more about a noun. Words such as fat, beautiful, good, bad etc. tell us more about any noun or a pronoun.

INTRODUCTION

We all know that adjectives are describing words. A word that tells us more about a noun or a pronoun is called adjective. For example, in the sentence- A thin man , the word 'thin' tells more about that man apart from the fact that he is a man.

Take another example where we see a cat, we say that the cat is cute, the word cute tells us more about that cat or we can say it helps us to know more about that particular cat.

Or when we say an angry man we mean that the man is angry.

A thin man

A cute cat

An **angry** man

Hot tea

Possessive Adjectives–Words like my, your, its, his and her tell us that something belongs to someone. They are called possessive adjectives. Words like our, your, and their show that something belongs to more than one person or group of people.

My House

Our house

Adjectives can also be used to compare two or more people, things or feelings. When we compare two things it is called comparative degree. We add 'er' to the word like 'cold' becomes 'colder'

Tall Taller Tallest

big, bigger, biggest

Remember

*The opposite words of adjectives are also adjective

Opposite words

Good	Bad
Happy	sad
Domestic	Wild
Hard	Soft
Brave	Timid
Tiny	Huge
Hot	Cold
Small	Big
Polite	Rude
Smooth	Rough
lever	Foolish
Laugh	Weep
Worst	Best

In some cases where the adjective ends in a 'y' we replace 'y' with 'ier'. **For example**: Nasty becomes nastier.

When we use adjectives to compare more than two people or things or feelings, it is called superlative degree. We add 'est' to a word to make it superlative degree.

Multiple Choice Question

LEVEL – 1

Directions (Qs. 1–10): Identify the adjective which describes the picture. Choose the answers from the options given below.

1. (a) Tall (b) Beautiful (c) Small (d) Big

2. (a) Big (b) Tall (c) Small (d) Short

3. (a) Thin (b) Fat (c) Tall (d) Small

4. (a) Happy (b) Famous (c) Angry (d) Sick

5. (a) Nice (b) Poor (c) Happy (d) Bad

6. (a) Painful (b) Hungry (c) Sleepy (d) Beautiful

7. (a) Weak   (b) Strong   (c) Happy   (d) Funny

8. (a) Ugly   (b) Big   (c) Kind   (d) Cute

9. (a) Cold   (b) Light   (c) Merry   (d) Short

10. (a) Happy   (b) Scared   (c) Angry   (d) Lovely

Directions (Qs. 11-15) : Give the opposites of the underlined adjectives by choosing the correct option.

11. Not all animals are <u>domestic</u>.

(a) wild   (b) tame   (c) game   (d) pet

12. She is a <u>happy</u> girl.

(a) joyful   (b) sad   (c) smile   (d) none

13. King Alexander was known to be <u>brave</u>.

(a) gallant   (b) strong   (c) timid   (d) silly

14. The ant is a <u>tiny</u> insect.   **(2013)**

(a) small   (b) huge   (c) less   (d) little

15. The teddy bear is very <u>soft</u>.

(a) smooth   (b) rough   (c) light   (d) hard

Directions (Qs. 16-20) : Choose the correct option.

16. Which of the following is not an adjective? (2012)

   (a) tall   (b) short   (c) come   (d) wide

17. Which of the following decribes a person?

   (a) brown   (b) green   (c) tall   (d) narrow

18. Which of the following adjective describes an animal?

   (a) wild   (b) bumpy   (c) square   (d) yellow

19. Which of the following words describes food? (2014)

   (a) oval   (b) sweet   (c) close   (d) none

20. Which of the following words describes shapes?

   (a) huge   (b) round   (c) soft   (d) light

21. I can't stand when somebody is _______ . (2021)
   (a) happily   (b) stay
   (c) joy   (d) rude

22. Manisha is _______ rude to everyone. (2022)
   (a) very   (b) much
   (c) lot   (d) more

LEVEL - 2

Directions (Qs. 1-5): Read the sentences given below and tell the adjectives from the options given below.

1.   I can see that Neha is very kind.
   (a)   very   (b)   Neha   (c)   see   (d)   kind

2.   Tim saved two puppies from falling down. (2013)
   (a)   Tim   (b)   saved   (c)   two   (d)   puppies

3.   Ruhi is a lazy girl; she will not finish her work on time.
   (a)   Ruhi   (b)   lazy   (c)   girl   (d)   finish

4.   We should never drink dirty water, it makes you fall sick.
   (a)   should   (b)   never   (c)   drink   (d)   dirty

5.   There are thirty students in my class
   (a)   there   (b)   are   (c)   thirty   (d)   students

Directions (Qs. 6-10): Fill in the blanks with the opposites of the underlined words choosing from the options given below.

6.   This room is <u>small</u>, I want a _____ room. (2016)

   (a)   big   (b)   bigger   (c)   small   (d)   little

7. **I found the test to be <u>easy</u> whereas Ram found it_____**

    (a) easy   (b) small   (c) difficult   (d) long

8. **Rahul is very <u>polite</u> but his brother is _____.**

    (a) rude   (b) noisy   (c) shy   (d) kind

9. **The <u>clever</u> fox fooled the _____ crow.**   **(2015)**

    (a) wise   (b) foolish   (c) intelligent   (d) honest

10. **Gandhiji always spoke the <u>truth</u> he never _____**

    (a) lied   (b) fooled   (c) planned   (d) behaved

Directions (Qs. 11–15): Fill in the blanks with correct adjectives from the options given below.   **[Critical Thinking]**

11. **The lion was so _____ that it started eating vegetables.**

    (a) brave   (b) kind   (c) wise   (d) hungry

12. **We all know that _____ always pays.**   **(2017)**

    (a) kindness   (b) honesty   (c) greatness   (d) warmth

13. **Ashoka was a _____ king. He is known for his victories.**

    (a) bad   (b) great   (c) kind   (d) ferocious

14. **He brought dark chocolates from France, They were _____ in taste.**

    (a) sweet   (b) salty   (c) big   (d) bitter

15. **I burnt my hand when I touched the _____plate.**

    (a) cold   (b) freezy   (c) icey   (d) hot

Directions (Qs. 16-20): Fill in the blanks with Comparative degree of adjectives, choosing the answers from the options given below.

16. **He is so good in maths but _____ in English.**

    (a) gooder   (b) goodest   (c) better   (d) best

17. **Ram is _____ than Shyam.**

    (a) tall   (b) tallest   (c) taller   (d) fit

18. **Her dress is _____ than mine.**

    (a) costliest   (b) costlier   (c) cost   (d) cheap

19. **The Hare ran _____ than the tortoise.**

    (a) fast   (b) faster   (c) fastest   (d) slow

20. **I can't carry my bag, it is _____ than yours.**

    (a) heavy   (b) heaviest   (c) heavier   (d) light

Directions (Qs. 21-22): Read the passage and choose the answer from the options given below.

Most people love to read books. Books are man's best friend. There are a large variety of books available in the market. Earlier books were available on rent. Now they are not available on rent. One, who reads a lot of books, has a rich vocabulary as well as good command over the language.

21.   How many adjectives have been used in this passage?

    (a)   one   (b)   four   (c)   three   (d)   ten

22.   What is the antonym of best?

    (a)   better   (b)   good   (c)   worse   (d)   worst

Directions (Qs. 23-24): Read the passage carefully and fill in the blanks from the options given below.

Lona lion was a very (23)________lion .All the animals in the jungle were (24) ________ of him. The moment they came to know that he was on a prowl, they would hide in their houses, and would not come out for days.

23.   (a)   big   (b)   ferocious   (c)   brave   (d)   small

24.   (a)   kind   (b)   happy   (c)   scared   (d)   silent

Directions (Qs. 25-29) : Read the sentences carefully and choose the correct option.

25.   Which adjective in bold print is used correctly?

    (a)   Seema is the **taller** girl in the class.   (b) Rita is **fastest** than Grace.

    (c)   Rita is the **older** of the two girls.   (d)   Sheenu is the **younger** girl on the team.

26.   Which adjective in Bold print tells colour?

    (a)   Do you see that **tiny** flower?   (b)   It has a **long** neck.

    (c)   Can you see its **two** wings?   (d)   I think its feathers are **green**.

27.   Which adjective in bold print tells size?

    (a)   I found a **large** rock in the dirt.   (b)   The rock was **round**.

    (c)   **Some** beads were next to the rock.   (d)   The beads were **white**.

28.   Which adjective in bold print tells shape?

    (a)   We saw a **little** animal in the bushes.   (b)   It had **brown** fur.

    (c)   Its eyes were **round**.   (d)   Its **four** legs shook with fright.

29. Which adjective in **bold** print tells how something sounds?
(a) Can you guess what is in the **little** cage? (b) It has a **long** tail.
(c) It makes **squeaky** noise.   (d) Its fur is **very** soft.

30. I bought _________ picture on the wall just here.   (2018)

(a) this   (b) that   (c) these   (d) those

31. I can see the _________ leaves on the tree from here.   (2018)

(a) flat, green   (b) bigger than   (c) as different as   (d) smaller than

32. The football match was so ______. I couldn't sleep afterwards.   (2018)

(a) excitable   (b) excited   (c) exciting   (d) excitably

33. These stones are the __________ things, I've ever seen.   (2018)

(a) rare   (b) rarer   (c) rarely   (d) rarest

34. This is a __________ stone.   (2019)

(a) high   (b) low   (c) big   (d) correctly

35. My mother didn't _________ me to go to the party.   (2020)
(a) allow   (b) allowed   (c) allowing   (d) allows

36. My grandfather prefers to listen to _______ music.   (2022)
(a) big   (b) thick   (c) soft   (d) interested

RESPONSE GRID

LEVEL 1

1. a b c d   2. a b c d   3. a b c d   4. a b c d   5. a b c d
6. a b c d   7. a b c d   8. a b c d   9. a b c d   10. a b c d
11. a b c d   12. a b c d   13. a b c d   14. a b c d   15. a b c d
16. a b c d   17. a b c d   18. a b c d   19. a b c d   20. a b c d
21. a b c d   22. a b c d

LEVEL 2

1. a b c d   2. a b c d   3. a b c d   4. a b c d   5. a b c d
6. a b c d   7. a b c d   8. a b c d   9. a b c d   10. a b c d
11. a b c d   12. a b c d   13. a b c d   14. a b c d   15. a b c d
16. a b c d   17. a b c d   18. a b c d   19. a b c d   20. a b c d

21. ⓐ ⓑ ⓒ ⓓ   22. ⓐ ⓑ ⓒ ⓓ   23. ⓐ ⓑ ⓒ ⓓ   24. ⓐ ⓑ ⓒ ⓓ   25. ⓐ ⓑ ⓒ ⓓ

26. ⓐ ⓑ ⓒ ⓓ   27. ⓐ ⓑ ⓒ ⓓ   28. ⓐ ⓑ ⓒ ⓓ   29. ⓐ ⓑ ⓒ ⓓ   30. ⓐ ⓑ ⓒ ⓓ

31. ⓐ ⓑ ⓒ ⓓ   32. ⓐ ⓑ ⓒ ⓓ   33. ⓐ ⓑ ⓒ ⓓ   34. ⓐ ⓑ ⓒ ⓓ   35. ⓐ ⓑ ⓒ ⓓ

36. ⓐ ⓑ ⓒ ⓓ

Solutions with Explanation

LEVEL – 1

1. **(b)** Beautiful, the flower is indeed beautiful to look at!
2. **(b)** Tall. giraffe is believed to be tall, it has a long neck.
3. **(b)** Fat   4. **(c)** Angry   5. **(b)** Poor
6. **(a)** Painful   7. **(b)** Strong   8. **(d)** Cute
9. **(a)** Cold   10. **(b)** Scared   11. **(a)** wild
12. **(b)** sad   13. **(c)** timid   14. **(b)** huge
15. **(d)** hard   16. **(c)** come   17. **(c)** tall
18. **(a)** wild   19. **(b)** sweet   20. **(b)** round
21. **(d)** I can't stand when somebody is rude.
22. **(a)** Very is used as quantity adverb

LEVEL – 2

1. **(d)** kind   2. **(c)** two   3. **(b)** lazy
4. **(d)** dirty   5. **(c)** thirty
6. **(a)** This room is small, but I want a big room.
7. **(c)** I found the test to be easy whereas Ram found it difficult.
8. **(a)** Rahul is very polite but his brother is rude.
9. **(b)** The clever fox fooled the foolish crow.
10. **(a)** Gandhiji always spoke the truth he never lied.
11. **(d)** The lion was so hungry that it started eating vegetables.
12. **(b)** It's an old proverb that says "Honesty always pays".
13. **(b)** Ashoka was a great king . He is known for his victories.
14. **(d)** He brought dark chocolates from France, They were bitter in taste. Dark chocolates are bitter in taste.
15. **(d)** I burnt my hand when I touched the hot plate.
16. **(c)** He is so good in maths but better in English. The comparative of good is better.
17. **(c)** Ram is taller than Shyam.
18. **(b)** Her dress is costlier than mine
19. **(b)** The Hare ran faster than the tortoise.

20. (c) Here heavier is comparison between two things so we use comparative degree.
21. (b) Four; best, large, rich, good
22. (d) Antonyms are opposite words. The opposite of best would be worst . As best is the superlative degree of good so worst is the superlative degree of bad.
23. (b) With lion we add the word ferocious.
24. (c) When someone is ferocious everyone around would be scared.
25. (c)
26. (d)
27. (a)
28. (c)
29. (c)
30. (a) that
31. (a) flat, green
32. (c) exciting
33. (d) rarest
34. (c) big
35. (a) allow
36. (c) My grandfather prefers to listen to soft music.

In this chapter, you will learn about 'adverbs'. These are the words which give some more information about the 'action words' or verbs used in the sentence.

Here is an exercise for you.

Directions: Underline the adverbs in the following sentences. Make new sentences from them using the picture clues.

1. The dog was barking loudly.

____

____

2. The child was crying fearfully.

____

____

3. Ramesh was dressed smartly.

____

____

4. Radhika was holding the trophy happily.

____

____

5. The crowd was cheering the Indian team joyfully

____

____

6. Ram waved goodbye to his friends tearfully.

____

____

7. The elephant ran wildly across the park.

____

____

6

Chapter

Adverbs

This lesson will help you to

*   understand adverbs.
*   use adverbs before verbs and adjectives.

INTRODUCTION

Adverbs are words that tell us something more about a verb or an adjective. Adverbs give us more information about a word and also change it slightly. For example, when we say that a boy suddenly started running. The word suddenly tells us how the boy started running.

Adverbs answer the following questions

*   How?
*   When?
*   Where?
*   Why?
*   How much?

ADVERBS OF HOW

Angrily	Suddenly	Slowly	Quietly
Quickly	Happily	Cheerfully	Jerkily
Sadly	Continuously	Badly	Softly
Gently			

Tell us how the action is done.

For example : The car ran jerkily on the road. How did the car run?

The cat came into the room slowly to catch the mouse. How did the cat come?

The words jerkily and slowly tell us how the action is being done.

❖ When we add 'ly' to a word it becomes an adverb.

For example: Slow becomes slowly.

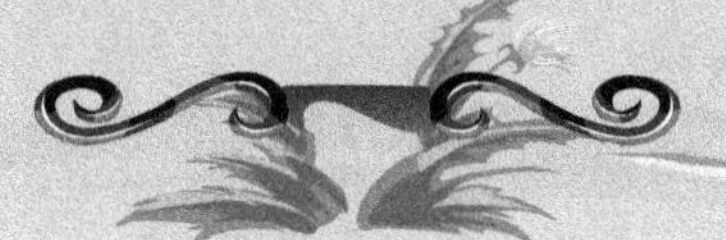

❖ Though most of the adverbs end with a 'ly' but there are some that do not end with 'ly'.

For example: Today, Seldom

The car ran **jerkily**.

The cat entered the room **slowly**.

ADVERBS OF FREQUENCY

Always	Never	Seldom	Often

He always goes to school. I seldom eat ice cream

Adverbs of Frequency tell us how often the action is done.

For example: He always goes to school.

How often does he go to school? **Always** answers the question.

I seldom eat ice creams.

How often you eat ice cream? **Seldom** answers the question.

ADVERBS OF QUANTITY

Quite	Very	Fully	Almost
Absolutely	Entirely	Rather	

The adverbs of quantity tell us how much?

For example: The car accident almost crashed the cars.

Here the word **almost** tells us the quantity of damage .

ADVERBS OF PLACE

Here	There	Upstairs	Downstairs
Nowhere			

Adverbs of place tell us where the action is done.

For example: a man is standing outside his car. The word outside tells us where the action is being done or is to be done.

The car accident almost crashed the cars.

A man standing outside his car.

Multiple Choice Question

LEVEL – 1

Directions (Qs. 1-10): Read the following sentences and fill in the blanks from the options given below.

1. _______ he got up and rushed to school.
   (a) Slowly   (b) Suddenly   (c) Happy   (d) True

2. Whatever you said is not new, I have heard this _____.
   (a) slowly   (b) before   (c) after   (d) never

3. She called me _______ to come over for tea   **(2012)**
   (a) twice   (b) never   (c) everywhere   (d) sadly

4. Can you please come _____ , the boss is waiting for you.
   (a) go   (b) in   (c) out   (d) suddenly

5. He _______ goes there. Nobody has seen him there.
   (a) never   (b) always   (c) happily   (d) slowly

6. Can you please stand ____. This is the queue.   **(2013)**
   (a) here   (b) there   (c) nowhere   (d) wherever

7. We all looked _____ at the sky to see the rainbow.
   (a) up   (b) looked   (c) down   (d) backwards

8. She talked to me very _____.
   (a) rude   (b) rudely   (c) suddenly   (d) fast

9. She changed her clothes _____ to get ready for the party.   **(2016)**
   (a) fastly   (b) quickly   (c) brightly   (d) cowardly

10. Tipu Sultan fought ___________ against the British.   **(2015)**
    (a) safely   (b) courageously   (c) softly   (d) suddenly

Directions (Qs. 11-15) : Fill in the blanks with suitable adverbs. Choose from the options.

11. The old lady walked _______ with the help of a stick.

(a) safely   (b) fast   (c) slowly   (d) clearly

12. Anna is _______ busy over the phone. (2015)

(a) outside (b) happily (c) rapidly (d) always

13. The man though fat, ran _______. (2013)

(a) fast (b) speedily (c) continuously (d) fastly

14. The soldiers fought _______.

(a) greedily (b) bravely (c) boldly (d) quickly

15. I brush my teeth _______ everyday.

(a) sometimes (b) twice (c) often (d) never

Directions (Qs. 16-20) : Read the questions carefully and choose the correct option.

16. Which of the following adverb talks about time? (2012)

    (a) Tia sleepily ate her lunch   (b) The movie started late

    (c) I stared at her coldly   (d) John gladly donated to charity

17. Identify the adverb that refers to feelings. (2014)

    (a) Anna treats everyone kindly   (b) The ocean is always wet

    (c) Flowers never talk   (d) It is sometimes cloudy

18. Identify the adverb that refers to sound.

    (a) The dog ate quickly   (b) Cats meow a lot

    (c) Ram ran quickly   (d) The children sat in the class quietly

19. Identify the adverb that refers to looks. (2016)

    (a) They easily finished the pizza   (b) She arrived today

    (c) Ram dresses smartly   (d) Faye exercises everyday.

20. Identify the adverb that refers to place (2013)

    (a) The dog jumped playfully   (b) She usually studies upstairs

    (c) Cheetas can run rapidly.   (d) The letter arrived today

21. My sister always eats really _________ . (2018)

    (a) slow   (b) slower   (c) slowest   (d) slowly

22. My mother always talks very _________ because she is very busy. (2019)

    (a) quicker   (b) quickly   (b) quickest   (d) quicken

23. Which of these is a feeling? (2021)

    (a) Happiness   (b) Stars

    (c) Road   (d) Question

LEVEL - 2

Directions (Qs. 1–5) Read the passage given below and fill in the blanks choosing the answers from the options given below (Tricky)

Ram was a very good boy. He (1)_______ obeyed his elders. He would not do any work without taking permission from his elder sister, Mom or Dad. He (2) ______ did anything without taking their permission. One day when he had gone out to play with his friends, one of his friends came there, eating an ice cream. Ram also wanted to have ice cream. He (3)________ ran back home , he asked his mom to give him money to buy an ice cream. His Mom refused. She said" You cannot have an ice cream as it is cold, and you will catch cold" . This disappointed Ram . But he did not lose hope. He (4)_____ went to his Dad. His Dad also refused to buy him an ice cream. Ram was very sad. He did not go back to the park to play, that day. He was so sad that he did not do his homework either. His Mom came to call him for dinner, but Ram (5)_____refused. This worried his mom.

1. (a) never   (b) always   (c) often   (d) seldom
2. (a) never   (b) often   (c) always   (d) seldom
3. (a) slowly   (b) hurriedly   (c) suddenly   (d) quietly
4. (a) fast   (b) slowly   (c) quickly   (d) continuously
5. (a) simply   (b) continuously   (c) suddenly   (d) softly

6. **Why do you think Ram's parents did not want to buy him an ice-cream?**

    (a) because, they were concerned about his health.

    (b) because, they did not want to spend money.

    (c) because, they did not like ice creams

    (d) because, they were in the habit of saying 'No'

Directions (Qs. 7-16): Look at the pictures and fill in the blanks with suitable adverbs. Choose the answers from the options given below

7. **The tortoise ran so ______ that it lost the race.**   **(2015)**

    (a) quietly   (b) slowly   (c) powerfully   (d) fastly

8. **Sam played the tune ______.**

    (a) quickly   (b) bravely   (c) rapidly   (d) nicely

9. **The mouse _______ nibbled away the biscuit.** (2016)
   (a) happily　　(b) slowly　　(c) quietly　　(d) carelessly

10. **We must speak _______ otherwise it sounds rude.** (2014)
    (a) slowly　　(b) quietly　　(c) politely　　(d) happily

11. **He played the music very ______.** (2013)
    (a) loudly　　(b) softly　　(c) melodiously　(d) smoothly

12. **Riya cut the cake __________.** (2017)
    (a) happily　　(b) sadly　　(c) slowly　　(d) quietly

13. **The boy sat ______ as his friend didn't give him a lollypop.** (2014)
    (a) quietly　　(b) slowly　　(c) sadly　　(d) softly

14. **Gina said to Yuvi. "______ go and sit there",**
    (a) happily　　(b) noisily　　(c) courageously　(d) quietly

15. **The car went _____ on the rugged plains.**
    (a) jerkily　　(b) smoothly　　(c) nicely　　(d) softly

16. We must _______ miss our school, unless we are unwell.   **(2017)**

   (a) always   (b) sometimes   (c) never   (d) often

Directions (Qs. 17-21): Read the following passage and fill in the blanks from the options given below.   **(Tricky, 2014)**

Siya was a very careless girl. She would keep her things (17) __________, and forget where she had kept them. One day her mother gave her some important papers, to keep them at a safe place. Siya was looking for a safe place in her room; (18) ________ the doorbell rang. The doorbell was ringing (19)_______. Siya kept the papers on her bed and (20)_________ ran to open the door. It was the postman, who was ringing the doorbell. She took the letter that he had got, and forgot about the papers. She went to the other room and started watching T.V. After watching T.V for a long time , she went back to her room, and slept till late in the evening. In the evening, when her mom asked for the papers. She had no idea, she (21) ______ran to her room to look for those papers , but could not find them.

17. (a) careful   (b) caring   (c) carelessly   (d) care

18. (a) slowly   (b) quickly   (c) suddenly   (d) fast.

19. (a) quitely   (b) slowly   (c) growingly   (d) continuously

20. (a) hurriedly   (b) completely   (c) quietly   (d) rushingly

21. (a) quickly   (b) unintentionally (c) continuously (d) suddenly

Directions (Qs. 22): Look at the grid below and tell how many adverbs are there, choose the answer from the options given below.   **(Critical Thinking)**

s	n	s	s	q
u	e	l	e	u
d	v	o	l	i
d	e	w	d	c
e	r	l	o	k
n	y	y	m	l
l	o	n	h	y
y	f	a	s	t

22. (a) 2   (b) 4   (c) 6   (d) 5

Directions (Qs. 23–30): Read the following sentences and identify adverbs. Choose answers from the options given below.

23. He seldom goes to his factory.
    (a) he   (b) seldom   (c) factory   (d) goes

24. He listened to me very patiently.   (2012)
    (a) listened   (b) to   (c) patiently   (d) me

25. The cat slyly ate the shares of both the monkeys.   (2015)
    (a) cat   (b) slyly   (c) shares   (d) both

26. We should now begin our homework.
    (a) should   (b) begin   (c) now   (d) homework

27. Nina would surely attend the class.   (2013)
    (a) would   (b) surely   (c) attend   (d) class

28. He went inside to see if someone was there in the room
    (a) went   (b) inside   (c) see   (d) there.

29. He carelessly kept the papers.   (2016)
    (a) carelessly   (b) he   (c) kept   (d) papers

30. She walked very gracefully to receive her trophy.
    (a) walked   (b) gracefully   (c) receive   (d) trophy

Directions (Qs. 31–35) Read the sentences and choose the opposite adverb.

31. The witch gave a pat <u>kindly</u>.
    (a) Caringly   (b) Critically   (c) Angrily   (d) Cruelly

32. The snail is moving <u>slowly</u>.   (2017)
    (a) Bravely   (b) Politely   (c) Kindly(d)   Quickly

33. The wind blew <u>softly</u> on my hair.   (2012)
    (a) Featherly   (b) Harshly   (c) Kindly(d)   Quickly

34. The children are playing <u>happily</u>.   (2015)
    (a) Sadly   (b) Loudly   (c) Patiently   (d) Slowly

35. The bride was dressed <u>beautifully</u>.   (2014)
    (a) Cruely   (b) Badly   (c) Gladly   (d) Dryly

36. The picture has ______ been seen by the public, so it was a mystery to everyone.   (2018)
    (a) never   (b) ever   (c) sometime   (d) proven

37. Teacher: Answer this question __________ to win the quiz.   (2021)
    (a) fastly   (b) fast
    (c) under   (d) off

RESPONSE GRID

LEVEL 1

1. a b c d 2. a b c d 3. a b c d 4. a b c d 5. a b c d
6. a b c d 7. a b c d 8. a b c d 9. a b c d 10. a b c d
11. a b c d 12. a b c d 13. a b c d 14. a b c d 15. a b c d
16. a b c d 17. a b c d 18. a b c d 19. a b c d 20. a b c d
21. a b c d 22. a b c d 23. a b c d

LEVEL 2

1. a b c d 2. a b c d 3. a b c d 4. a b c d 5. a b c d
6. a b c d 7. a b c d 8. a b c d 9. a b c d 10. a b c d
11. a b c d 12. a b c d 13. a b c d 14. a b c d 15. a b c d
16. a b c d 17. a b c d 18. a b c d 19. a b c d 20. a b c d
21. a b c d 22. a b c d 23. a b c d 24. a b c d 25. a b c d
26. a b c d 27. a b c d 28. a b c d 29. a b c d 30. a b c d
31. a b c d 32. a b c d 33. a b c d 34. a b c d 35. a b c d
36. a b c d 37. a b c d

Solutions with Explanation

LEVEL – 1

1. **(b)** Suddenly he got up and rushed to school

2. **(b)** Whatever you said is not new, I have heard this before.

3. **(a)** She called me twice to come over for tea

4. **(b)** Can you please come in , the boss is waiting for you.

5. **(a)** He never goes there . Nobody has seen him there.

6. **(a)** Can you please stand here. This is the queue.

7. **(a)** We all looked up at the sky to see the rainbow.

8. **(b)** She talked to me very rudely.

9. **(b)** She changed her clothes quickly to get ready for the party.

10. **(b)** Tipu Sultan fought courageously, against the british.

11. **(c)** slowly   12 **(d)** always   13. **(d)** fastly   14. **(b)** bravely

15. **(b)** twice   16. **(b)**   17. **(a)**   18. **(b)**

19. (c)   20. (b)

21. (d) slowly

22. (b) quickly

23. (a) From the given options Happiness is a feeling.

LEVEL – 2

1.   (b) always   2.   (a) never   3.   (b) hurriedly

4.   (c) quickly   5.   (d) softly

6.   (a) because, they were concerned about his health.

7.   (b) The tortoise ran so slowly that it lost the race.

8.   (d) Sam played the tune nicely.

9.   (b) The mouse slowly nibbled away the biscuit. Nibbling means, eating slowly.

10. (c) We must always speak politely, We must never disrespect anyone

11. (a) He played the music very loudly.

12. (a) Riya cut the cake happily.

13. (c) The boy sat sadly as his friend didn't give him a lollypop.

14. (d) Gina said to Yuvi. "quietly go and sit there",

15. (a) The car went jerkily on the rugged plains.

16. (c) We must never miss our school, unless we are unwell.

17. (c) carelessly   18. (c) suddenly   19. (d) continuously

20. (a) hurriedly   21. (a) quickly

22. (c) 6; suddenly, seldom, fast, never, quickly, slowly

23. (b) seldom   24. (c) patiently   25. (b) slyly

26. (c) now   27. (b) surely   28. (b) inside

29. (a) carelessly   30. (b) gracefully   31. (d) cruelly

32. (d) Quickly   33. (b) Harshly   34. (a) Sadly

35. (b) Badly

36. (a) never

37. (b) Answer this question fast to win the quiz.

The topic of this chapter is 'preposition'. As its name indicates, preposition tells about the position of persons or things we are talking about. You will know about the usage of prepositions in detail in this chapter.

Here is an exercise for you.

Directions: Prepositions link nouns or pronouns to other words in a sentence. Read the sentences given below and use prepositions in the box to fill in the blanks.

around, about, at, by, into, for, after, off

1. Garima has breakfast _____________ 9:00 A.M.

2. In Delhi, people like to travel _____________ the metro.

3. The students are sitting _____________ the teacher.

4. People are talking _____________ the incident.

5. The nail came_____________ the wall.

6. We are going to Chennai _____________ 25th of May.

7. My mother brought me a wrist watch _____________ five thousand rupees.

8. Raghav dived_____________ the swimming pool.

7

Chapter

Prepositions

LEARNING OBJECTIVES

This lesson will help you to

- learn the correct way to use prepositions.
- identify prepositions

INTRODUCTION

Prepositions are also known as "Where" words. They tell us about the position of a person or a thing or time of an action.

Here are some common prepositions.

At is used for small towns, as well as time.

For example: I will leave at 5 in the evening.

Words like on, at, by, for, past tell us about time.

For example: He left at half past twelve.

In is used for large cities or countries.

For example: I am a native of India but stay in France.

On is used for smaller places.

For example: I am sitting on a chair.

Among is used when we talk of many objects or people. **For example:** He is among the best students of the school.

Between is used when we talk of two things or people. **For example:** The police van got stuck between two buildings.

By is used when we talk of a person doing something. **For example:** He is going by car.

With is used when we talk of a tool used by a person.

For example: A boy is writing with a pencil.

With can also be used to show company of.

For example: Sheena went for cycling with her friends.

A boy is writing with a pencil.

Sheena went for cycling with her friends.

We use **Since** when we talk of a fixed time.

We use **For** when we want to show a period of time.

For example: For how long have you been working here?

Besides means in addition to.

For example: Besides he was quite hungry.

Beside means by the side of.

For example: Harry was standing beside me.

Harry was standing beside me.

Do You Know:

❖ Preposition of manner is all about how a certain thing happened or is done.

Ex: On, By, With, Like etc.

Remember

❖ The Preposition 'with' is used in different ways. It is used to show 'using' for example: Tom is playing with his ball. With can also be used to mean together with or in company of.

Multiple Choice Questions

LEVEL – 1

Directions (Qs. 1-10): Read the sentences and fill in the blanks from the options given below

1. The little girl has been hiding ______ the table.

   (a) over   (b) under   (c) above   (d) on

2. It is so hot, the sun is almost ______ our heads.   **(2015)**

   (a) above   (b) under   (c) in   (d) on

3. Tim lay down ______ the grass.

   (a) in   (b) on   (c) above   (d) over

4. I saw a rainbow ______ the sky.

   (a) in   (b) on   (c) over   (d) above

5. Why are you so late? It's half ______seven.   **(2017)**

   (a) past   (b) on   (c) at   (d) in

6. My dad comes home ______six o' clock.

   (a) past   (b) at   (c) in   (d) on

7. Always wash your hands ___soap before you eat.   **(2016)**

   (a) at   (b) in   (c) with   (d) on

8. The bag is ___ the sofa.

   (a) above   (b) in   (c) on   (d) with

9. Why are you hiding ______the chair?

   (a) over   (b) in   (c) behind   (d) on

10. Where is the ball? Is it ______ the table?

    (a) above   (b) over   (c) on   (d) under

Directions (Q. No. 11-15) : Read the following questions and choose the correct option.

11. Which of the following is a preposition?   **(2013)**

    (a) Beside   (b) Come   (c) Go   (d) Three

12. Which of the following preposition talks about manner?   **(2014)**

    (a) At   (b) With   (c) Across   (d) Towards

13. Identify the preposition of place. (2016)

(a) I forgot to wish you **on** your birthday.

(b) We were served food **with** soft drinks.

(c) I will meet you **at** the airport.

(d) Two seats were reserved **for** us.

14. Identify the preposition of time. (2015)

(a) He might see us **in** the evening.

(b) I was sitting **under** the tree.

(c) The train left **from** the platform 9.

(d) Did you call **at** my house?

15. Which of the following is not a preposition? (2013)

(a) Before   (b) Among   (c) Under   (d) Sing

Directions (Qs. 16-20) : Look at the pictures and find the correct sentence out of the following.

16. 

(a) The cake is in the oven.

(b) The cake is behind the oven.

(c) The cake is near the oven.

(d) The cake is between the oven.

17.   (2016)

(a) The pen is in the stand.

(b) The pen is to the stand.

(c) The pen is on the stand.

(d) The pen is infront of the stand.

18.

(a) The girl is standing in the boys. (b) The girl is standing between the boys.

(c) The girl is standing near the boys. (d) The girl is standing behind the boys.

19. **(2012)**

(a) The Sun is on the cloud. (b) The Sun is between the cloud.

(c) The Sun is in the cloud. (d) The Sun is behind the cloud.

20. **(2013)**

(a) The cat is next to the ball. (b) The cat is behind the ball.

(c) The cat is under the ball. (d) The cat is on the ball.

21. Why is there a difference ________ price for these shoes ? **(2018)**

(a) with (b) since (c) for (d) in

22. I found my lost earring ________ the rug. **(2021)**

(a) at (b) with

(c) under (d) in

23. My aunt lives _______a hospital. **(2022)**

(a) on (b) with

(c) from (d) near

Directions (Q. No. 24): Choose the corect option for the underlined word.

24. I was waiting for my friend <u>in</u> the park.   (2022)

    (a) Pronoun   (b) Preposition

    (c) Conjunction   (d) Adverb

Directions (Q. No. 25): Choose the correct option to fill in the blank.

25. I always go on morning walks _______ my mother.   (2022)

    (a) for   (b) with   (c) to   (d) into

26. Which one of the following options is correct for the picture shown below?

                                                                  (2022)

    (a) The old man is resting at the tree.   (b) The old man is resting to the tree.

    (c) The old man is resting on the tree.   (d) The old man is resting under the tree.

LEVEL – 2

Directions (Qs. 1–4): In the picture given below identify the prepositions and answer from the options given below.

  1. The girl is playing ____ sand.

    (a) on   (b) in   (c) over   (d) above

2. **The boy is playing _____his dad.**

    (a) on   (b) in   (c) with   (d) from

3. **The children are making castles ____sand.**

    (a) with   (b) over   (c) from   (d) under

4. **The boy is playing ____a ball in the pool.**

    (a) in   (b) with   (c) over   (d) from

Directions (Qs. 5-10): Read the sentences given below and recognize the prepositions. Choose the answers from the options given below

5. **See Rahul is sitting beside Ravi.**   (Tricky, 2012)

    (a) See   (b) Rahul   (c) sitting   (d) beside

6. **Reema's car has got stuck between the two trucks.**

    (a) Reema   (b) car   (c) got   (d) between

7. **He is among one of the best guitar players.**

    (a) He   (b) among   (c) best   (d) guitar

8. **When it came to choosing between a lie and truth, he chose truth.**   (2014)

    (a) When   (b) came   (c) choosing   (d) between

9. **He walked across the lane.**

    (a) He   (b) walked   (c) across.   (d) lane

10. **Look! there is an old man standing on the roof of the building.**   (2016)

    (a) Look   (b) there   (c) on   (d) standing

Directions (Qs. 11): Look at the grid below and tell how many prepositions have been used   [Critical Thinking]

w	b	e	s	i	d	e	s	j
i	k	u	n	d	e	r	j	n
t	w	h	q	e	t	i	l	m
h	b	e	t	w	e	e	n	k
l	n	t	r	g	p	o	t	n
k	a	b	o	v	e	v	l	y
h	m	m	n	f	s	n	k	o
o	n	b	c	j	a	b	n	c

11. (a) 4   (b) 8   (c) 6   (d) 7

Directions (Qs. 12-20): Read the passage given below and fill in the blanks from the options given below.   **(Tricky, 2012)**

The Thirsty Crow

Once upon a time there was a crow. It was very thirsty. So, it was looking for water (12) ____ here to there. But it could not find water anywhere. It went (13)____ the mountains to look for water, but the mountains were dry. It was hot summer season! It went and sat (14) ____ top of a mountain to be able to find water. (15)____ there it saw a group of crocodiles playing (16)___ water (17) ____ a pond. The crow was so thirsty, that it wanted to quickly fly there and drink water. But it knew that it was very difficult to have water (18) ____ there. The crocodiles will not let it drink water (19) ____ that pond. So, it thought of a plan. It flew away to that pond. After it reached there, it said" I had a dream yesterday, I saw God. God has sent me here to tell you a few things but separately not together". Actually it planned to create disunity (20) ____ the crocodiles.

12. (a) of   (b) with   (c) from   (d) above
13. (a) between   (b) above   (c) on   (d) under
14. (a) in   (b) on   (c) with   (d) at
15. (a) From   (b) Behind   (c) Under   (d) Below
16. (a) above   (b) at   (c) with   (d) on
17. (a) in   (b) on
    (c) at   (d) from
18. (a) with   (b) from
    (c) in   (d) on
19. (a) from   (b) above
    (c) under   (d) between
20. (a) of   (b) with
    (c) between   (d) among

Directions (Qs. 21–25): Look at the pictures given below and then choose the answer from the options given below

21. The boy is sitting ___ grass.

   (a)   in   (b)   on   (c)   at   (d)   above

22. The car got stuck ____snow.   (2015)

   (a)   in   (b)   on   (c)   of   (d)   for

23. The metro train is running _____ ground.

   (a)   on   (b)   above   (c)   up   (d)   at

24. The birds are flying ____the sky.   (2013)

   (a)   on   (b)   at   (c)   in   (d)   of

25. **The girl is playing ___the balloons.**

   (a) with   (b) at   (c) on   (d) from

Directions (Qs. 26): Find out the number of prepositions in the box given. Choose the answers from the options given below.   (Critical Thinking)

Behind	Because	should	past	at	into
mother	it	on	girl	camel	above,
he	she	cow	with		

26. (a) 9   (b) 7   (c) 10   (d) 5

27. **Match the following and choose the answers from the options given below**

A	Shreya ran	1	to divide land among themselves.
B	People who belong to India	2	on the track
C	Mother told her sons	3	speak in Hindi.
d	I was	4	at the restaurant

	A	B	C	D
(a)	4	3	2	1
(b)	2	3	1	4
(c)	3	4	1	2
(d)	4	1	2	3

Directions (Qs. 28–30): Read the passage given below and answer the questions from the options given below. (Tricky, 2015)

A Page from Rehan's Diary

I thought that dinosaurs have become extinct, but believe me; they haven't. I saw a dinosaur yesterday. It stood behind me, and patted me on my back. I looked back, it was a dinosaur! I was very scared. I wanted to jump up the tree. But it would not have been of much use. The dinosaur was bigger than that tree. I started running with all my might and sat under my car so that it is not able to see me.

28. Where was the dinosaur standing?

    (a) behind   (b) above   (c) under   (d) over

29. Where did Rehan want to go and hide?

    (a) jump up the tree   (b) jump over the tree

    (c) jump under the tree   (d) jump between the tree.

30. Is "under" a preposition?

    (a) Yes

    (b) No

    (c) May be

    (d) None of these

Directions (Qs. 31-35) : Choose the correct option after reading the sentence.

31. (a) The teacher congratulated me on my achievement.

    (b) The teacher congratulated me for my achievement.

    (c) The teacher congratulated me at my achievement.

    (d) The teacher congratulated me over my achievement.

32. (a) He left for Bengaluru with train. (2013)

    (b) He left for Bengaluru by train.

    (c) He left for Bengaluru on train.

    (d) He left for Bengaluru in train.

33. (a) Radha met Navin at her way to school.

(b) Radha met Navin by her way to school.

(c) Radha met Navin on her way to school.

(d) Radha met Navin in her way to school.

34. (a) He is an expert at making excuses. **(2015)**

(b) He is an expert from making excuses.

(c) He is an expert over making excuses.

(d) He is an expert in making excuses.

35. (a) There is no point in going to the market now.

(b) There is no point to go to the market now.

(c) There is no point by going to the market now.

(d) There is no point from going to the market now.

36. It will be delivered to you ________ two days at the most. **(2019)**

(a) with (b) on (c) out (d) in

37. The old man leaned _______ the table. **(2020)**

(a) up (b) against

(c) by (d) in

38. Rahul: Tell me about it. Don't beat ______ the bush. **(2021)**

Akki: Have patience.

(a) off (b) around

(c) near (d) beside

39. Boss Let's call ______ today's last meeting.

Manager: Ok, sir. **(2021)**

(a) of (b) at

(c) under (d) off

40. Sumit takes _____ his grandfather. **(2021)**

(a) on (b) after

(c) up (d) at

RESPONSE GRID

LEVEL 1

1. a b c d   2. a b c d   3. a b c d   4. a b c d   5. a b c d
6. a b c d   7. a b c d   8. a b c d   9. a b c d   10. a b c d
11. a b c d   12. a b c d   13. a b c d   14. a b c d   15. a b c d
16. a b c d   17. a b c d   18. a b c d   19. a b c d   20. a b c d
21. a b c d   22. a b c d   23. a b c d   24. a b c d   25. a b c d
26. a b c d

LEVEL 2

1. a b c d   2. a b c d   3. a b c d   4. a b c d   5. a b c d
6. a b c d   7. a b c d   8. a b c d   9. a b c d   10. a b c d
11. a b c d   12. a b c d   13. a b c d   14. a b c d   15. a b c d
16. a b c d   17. a b c d   18. a b c d   19. a b c d   20. a b c d
21. a b c d   22. a b c d   23. a b c d   24. a b c d   25. a b c d
26. a b c d   27. a b c d   28. a b c d   29. a b c d   30. a b c d
31. a b c d   32. a b c d   33. a b c d   34. a b c d   35. a b c d
36. a b c d   37. a b c d   38. a b c d   39. a b c d   40. a b c d

Solutions with Explanation

LEVEL – 1

1. **(b)** The little girl has been hiding under the table.

2. **(d)** It is so hot, the sun is almost on our heads.

3. **(b)** Tim lay down on the grass.

4. **(a)** I saw a rainbow in the sky.

5. **(a)** Why are you so late? It's half past seven.

6. **(b)** My dad comes home at six o' clock.

7. **(c)** Always wash your hands with soap before you start eating.

8. **(c)** The bag is on the sofa.

9. **(c)** Why are you hiding behind the chair?

10. **(d)** Where is the ball? Is it under the table?

11. **(a)** Beside

12. **(b)** With

13. **(c)** at

14. **(a)** in

15. **(d)** Sing

16. **(a)** The cake is in the oven.

17. **(c)** The pen is on the stand.

18. **(b)** The girl is standing between the boys.

19. **(d)** The sun is behind the cloud.

20. **(a)** The cat is next to the ball.

21. **(d)** in

22. **(c)** under

23. **(d)** My aunt lives near the hospital.

24. **(b)** In is an example of preposition. Other prepositions are at, on, beside etc.

25. **(b)** With is used to show togetherness in activity.

26. **(d)**

LEVEL – 2

1. **(b)** in	2. **(c)** with
3. **(a)** with	4. **(b)** with
5. **(d)** beside	6. **(d)** between
7. **(b)** among	8. **(d)** between
9. **(c)** across	10. **(c)** on

11. **(c)** 6; besides, between, on, with, above, under.

12. **(c)** from	13. **(b)** above
14. **(b)** on	15. **(a)** From
16. **(c)** with	17. **(a)** in
18. **(b)** from	19. **(a)** from

20. **(d)** among

21. **(b)** The boy is sitting on grass.

22. **(a)** The car got stuck in snow

23. **(b)** The metro train is running above ground.

24. **(c)** The birds are flying in the sky.

25. **(a)** The girl is playing with the balloons.

26. **(b)** Behind, at, Past, on Above, in, with

27. **(b)**

28. **(a)** behind

29. **(a)** jump up the tree

30. **(a)** under is a preposition

31. **(a)**

32. **(b)**

33. **(c)**

34. **(d)**

35. **(a)**

36. **(d)** in

37. **(b)** against

38. **(b)** Don't beat around the bush.

39. **(d)** Let's call off today's meeting.

40. **(b)** Sumit takes after his grandfather.

<table><tr><td>8</td><td></td></tr></table>

CHAPTER FOREWORD

In this chapter, you will learn about articles. In English, there are three articles – a, an and the.

This chapter discusses in detail how and when these articles are used in a sentence.

Here is an exercise for you which is based on usage of articles.

Directions: Choose the correct option.

1. There is ______________ in the bottle. Please drink it.

   (i)   a juice

   (ii)   juice

   (iii)   the juice

2. I like ______________ of this film.

   (i)   the music

   (ii)   a music

   (iii)   music

3. My grandmother makes ________________ just before the rains.

   (i)   mango pickles

   (ii)   the mango pickles

   (iii)   a mango pickles

4. The customer was not happy with __________________ .

   (i)   a curtain cloth

   (ii)   the curtain cloth

   (iii)   curtain cloth

Articles

LEARNING OBJECTIVES

This lesson will help you to

- learn articles.
- use articles to make proper sentences.

INTRODUCTION

As you know there are 26 letters in English alphabet. Out of them there are only five vowels, rest all are consonants. The five vowels are,a e, i, o, u. We use articles such as 'a', 'an' or 'the'.

Use of a:

A is used before the words that begin with a consonant sound.

For example: a boy, a girl, a cup, a clock, a butterfly, a star.

A boy   A girl   A cup

A clock   A butterfly   A star

Use of an:

An is used before words that begin with vowels... a, e, i, o, u. or a vowel sound.

For example: An ice-cream, an egg, an inkpot.

An ice-cream   An egg   An owl

 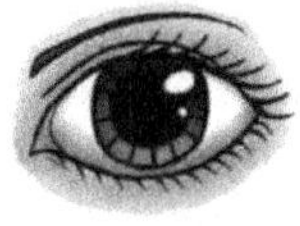 

An inkpot   An eye   An Ostrich

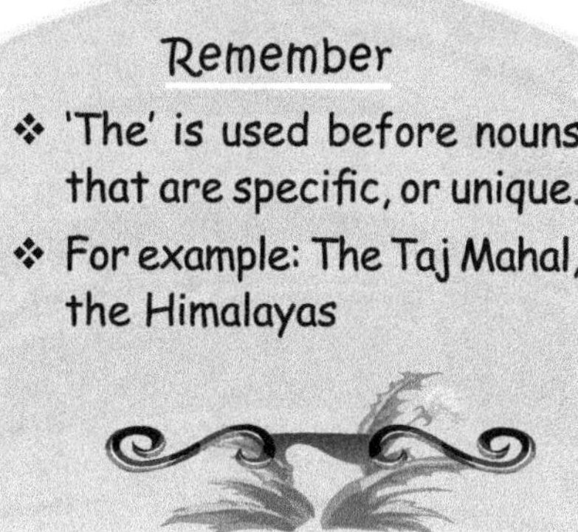

Use of the:

'The' is used before some particular person or things.

For example: The Himalayas, the Bible, the Sun.

The Qutub Minar   The Himalayas

The Sun   The Bible

A and An suggest any person or thing.

For example: A tree (any tree).

The tree that is near my house.

No article is used before proper nouns.

For example:

Mr. Smith is very hardworking.

Snoopy is the name of his pet dog.

Multiple Choice Questions

LEVEL - 1

Directions (Qs. 1–10): Fill in the blanks with appropriate article.

1. He gave me _______ twenty oranges to eat. They were all sour. **(2012)**
   (a) a   (b) an   (c) the   (d) None of these

2. He attends school every day. His class is on ______ second floor.
   (a) a   (b) an   (c) the   (d) None of these

3. You are late by _____ hour. You can't participate now. **(2014)**
   (a) a   (b) an   (c) the   (d) None of these

4. _____George Washington was a great person. He was the President of the USA.
   (2016)
   (a) A   (b) An   (c) The   (d) None of these

5. The Presidents of the U.S.A stay in ___ White House.
   (a) a   (b) an   (c) the   (d) None of these

6. Have you seen ___ India Gate? It's a nice place. **(2013)**
   (a) a   (b) an   (c) the   (d) None of these

7. Hurry! Otherwise we will miss ___ Movie
   (a) a   (b) an   (c) the   (d) None of these

8. Get _____ umbrella, it is raining outside.
   (a) a   (b) an   (c) the   (d) None of these

9. I want to eat ___ ice cream from that shop. **(2012)**
   (a) a   (b) an   (c) the   (d) None of these

10. ___ Earth revolves around the Sun in 365 days. **(2015)**
    (a) A   (b) An   (c) The   (d) None of these

Directions (Qs. 11–15) : Read the sentences carefully and choose the sentence with the correct use of article.

11. **(2013)**

   (a) I ate a mango in the morning.   (b) I ate the mango in a morning.
   (c) I ate an mango in the morning.   (d) I ate a mango in an morning.

12.    **(2012)**

(a) Fruits are in an basket.   (b) The fruits are in the basket.

(c) Fruits are in a basket.   (d) An fruits are in a basket.

13.    **(2015)**

(a) We live in a expensive home.   (b) We live in an expensive home.

(c) We live in the expensive home.   (d) All of the above are correct.

14.    **(2016)**

(a) I caught a fish from the lake.   (b) I caught the fish in a lake.

(c) I caught the fish in an lake.   (d) I caught fish in lake.

15. (a) A book you need is with me.   (b) An book you need is with me.

(c) The book you need is with me.   (d) Book you need is with me.

Directions (Qs. 16–20) : Look at the pictures and answer the following questions with the correct use of article.

16. What is on the table?

There is _____ flower vase on the table.

(a) a   (b) an   (c) the   (d) No article

17. Why is Agra famous? (2017)

Agra is famous for _______ Taj Mahal

(a) a (b) an (c) the (d) No article

18. Where does Jack work? (2016)

Jack works in .... restaurant.

(a) a (b) an (c) the (d) No article

19. What is the girl eating? (2012)

The girl is eating .... egg.

(a) a (b) an (c) the (d) No article

20. Where do wild animals live? (2014)

Wild animals live in _________ jungle.

(a) a (b) an (c) the (d) No article

21. **He always eats with _________ spoon and fork.** (2019)

    (a) an   (b) the   (c) a   (d) no article

22. **I met _______ European in the market.** (2021)
    (a) a   (b) an
    (c) the   (d) no article

23. **He is _______ naughtiest boy in our family.** (2022)
    (a) a   (b) the
    (c) an   (d) no article

24. **The boy is holding ______ orange in his hands.** (2022)

    (a) an   (b) a
    (c) x   (d) None of these

LEVEL – 2

Directions (Qs. 1–11): Read the passage carefully and fill in the blanks from the options given below (Critical Thinking, 2013)

Most Intelligent Man

Once upon ___(1) time, there was a man whose name was "Most intelligent". He had kept this name on his own. He always thought that there was no one in ___(2) world who could defeat him in intelligence. The story of his keeping his name 'Most intelligent' goes twenty years back. That time he was as normal as any other person, and his name was Diwakar, until he went to ___(3) temple. There ___(4) woman had lost her slippers. She was walking barefoot, and looking for her slippers. It was very hot, and ___(5) Sun was showing its full fury. It was very tough to walk on ___(6)hot floor. That woman got really troubled, and was calling for help. Diwakar came to help her. He started looking for her slippers. But could not find them. Diwakar was ___(7) cobbler by profession, he did not waste any time and made a pair of slippers in less than ___(8) hour . This really impressed all ___(9) people around. And ___(10) chorus voice came, "Diwakar is ___(11) most intelligent".

1.   (a) a   (b) an   (c) the   (d) None of these

2.	(a)	a	(b)	an	(c)	the	(d) None of these
3.	(a)	a	(b)	an	(c)	the	(d) None of these
4.	(a)	a	(b)	an	(c)	the	(d) None of these
5.	(a)	a	(b)	an	(c)	the	(d) None of these
6.	(a)	a	(b)	an	(c)	the	(d) None of these
7.	(a)	a	(b)	an	(c)	the	(d) None of these
8.	(a)	a	(b)	a	(c)	the	(d) None of these
9.	(a)	a	(b)	an	(c)	the	(d) None of these
10.	(a)	a	(b)	an	(c)	the	(d) None of these
11.	(a)	a	(b)	an	(c)	the	(d) None of these

Directions (Qs. 12–21): Look at the pictures and put articles choosing from the options given below

12.

   (a) A   (b) An   (c) The   (d) None of these

13.   **(2013)**

   (a) A   (b) An   (c) The   (d) None of these

14.

   (a) A   (b) An   (c) The   (d) None of these

15.  **(2014)**

(a)   A   (b)   An   (c)   The   (d)   None of these

16. 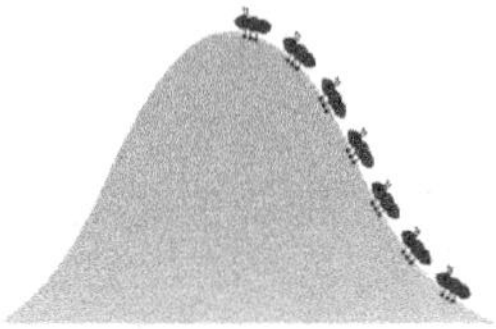 **(2012)**

(a)   A   (b)   An   (c)   The   (d)   None of these

17.  **(2014)**

(a)   A   (b)   An   (c)   The   (d)   None of these

18.  **(2015)**

(a)   A   (b)   An   (c)   The   (d)   None of these

19.  **(2012)**

(a)   A   (b)   An   (c)   The   (d)   None of these

20.

(a)   A   (b)   An   (c)   The   (d)   None of these

21.    **(2016)**

(a) A   (b) An   (c) The   (d) None of these

Directions (Qs. 22): Look at the box below and tell how many words need 'an' before them   **(Tricky)**

Igloo	soap	eraser	book	frog	pillow
ball	television	mango	coconut	carrot	milk

22. (a) 2   (b) 4   (c) 6   (d) 3

Directions (Qs. 23 to 30): Read the passage given below and answer the questions from the options given below.   **(Tricky, 2015)**

An Alien In Class.

It was Monday morning. All (23) _____ children were seated on their seats. (24) ___teacher took attendance. In the midst of all this (25) ___door opened , (26) ____ alien walked in. (27) ____ teacher did not notice that it was looking different from other children. The alien greeted (28) ______ teacher and sat down. All (29) ____ children were looking at that alien. After taking attendance (30) ___ teacher looked up.

23. (a) a   (b) an   (c) the   (d) None of these
24. (a) a   (b) An   (c) The   (d) None of these
25. (a) a   (b) an   (c) the   (d) None of these
26. (a) a   (b) an   (c) the   (d) None of these
27. (a) A   (b) An   (c) The   (d) None of these
28. (a) a   (b) an   (c) the   (d) None of these
29. (a) a   (b) an   (c) the   (d) None of these
30. (a) a   (b) an   (c) the   (d) None of these

31. This is ________ smallest cat I have ever seen.   **(2018)**

(a) a   (b) an   (c) the   (d) no article

32. My mother is waiting for ________ postman to deliver her magazines.   **(2020)**

(a) a   (b) an
(c) the   (d) no article

33. There was ________ leak on the roof but we could not find it.   **(2020)**

(a) a   (b) an   (c) the   (d) no article

RESPONSE GRID

LEVEL 1

1. a b c d   2. a b c d   3. a b c d   4. a b c d   5. a b c d
6. a b c d   7. a b c d   8. a b c d   9. a b c d   10. a b c d
11. a b c d   12. a b c d   13. a b c d   14. a b c d   15. a b c d
16. a b c d   17. a b c d   18. a b c d   19. a b c d   20. a b c d
21. a b c d   22. a b c d   23. a b c d   24. a b c d

LEVEL 2

1. a b c d   2. a b c d   3. a b c d   4. a b c d   5. a b c d
6. a b c d   7. a b c d   8. a b c d   9. a b c d   10. a b c d
11. a b c d   12. a b c d   13. a b c d   14. a b c d   15. a b c d
16. a b c d   17. a b c d   18. a b c d   19. a b c d   20. a b c d
21. a b c d   22. a b c d   23. a b c d   24. a b c d   25. a b c d
26. a b c d   27. a b c d   28. a b c d   29. a b c d   30. a b c d
31. a b c d   32. a b c d   33. a b c d

Solutions with Explanation

LEVEL - 1

1. **(d)** He gave me twenty oranges to eat. They were all sour.

2. **(c)** He attends school every day. His class is on the second floor

3. **(b)** You are late by an hour. You can't participate now.

4. **(d)** George Washington was a great person. He was the President of USA.

5. **(c)** The Presidents of the U.S.A stay in the White House.

6. **(c)** Have you seen the India Gate? It's a nice place.

7. **(c)** Hurry! Otherwise we will miss the Movie

8. **(b)** Get an umbrella, it is raining outside.

9. **(b)** I want to eat an ice cream from that shop.

10. **(c)** The Earth revolves around the Sun in 365 days..

11. **(a)** I ate a mango in the morning
12. **(c)** Fruits are in a basket.
13. **(b)** We live in an expensive home
14. **(a)** I cought a fish from the lake.
15. **(c)** The book you need is with me.
16. **(a)** a
17. **(c)** the
18. **(a)** a
19. **(b)** an
20. **(c)** the
21. **(c)** a
22. **(a)** I met a European in the market.
23. **(b)** 'The' is used with the superlative form of verb.
24. **(a)**

LEVEL – 2

1. **(a)** a	2. **(c) the**	3. **(a) a**	4. **(a) a**
5. **(c) the**	6. **(c) the**	7. **(a) a**	8. **(b) an**
9. **(c) the**	10. **(a) a**	11. **(c) the**	

12. **(c)** The Qutub Minar
13. **(a)** A bus. 'A' because it starts with a consonant 'b'
14. **(b)** An aeroplane. 'An' because it starts with a vowel 'a'
15. **(a)** A watermelon. 'a' because it starts with a consonant 'w'
16. **(b)** An anthill. An because it starts with a vowel 'a'. An anthill is a shelter built by ants for themselves.'
17. **(d)** Sugar is an uncountable noun so none of the articles can be used before it.
18. **(b)** An onion. 'An' because onion starts with a vowel 'o'
19. **(a)** A penguin. 'A' because it starts with a consonant 'p'.
20. **(a)** A rabbit. 'a' because it starts with a consonant 'r'.
21. **(b)** An ostrich. 'An' because it starts with a vowel 'o'.
22. **(a)** 2. Igloo, Eraser.

23. **(c)** the	24. **(c)** The	25. **(c)** the	26. **(b)** an
27. **(c)** The	28. **(c)** the	29. **(c)** the	30. **(c)** the

31. **(c)** the
32. **(c)** the
33. **(a)** a

9 # CHAPTER FOREWORD

This chapter deals with 'conjunctions' which are also called 'connecting words'. These words connect sentences and words.

Here is an exercise for you based on conjunctions.

Directions: Join sentences using appropriate conjunctions. Choose from the options provided in brackets.

1. Mr. Rajesh is very old _______________ he is physically very fit.   (and, so, but)
2. Deepak was late for office _______________ he was stuck in the traffic jam.
   (because, while, so)
3. _______________ Reema is fat, she can run fast.   (Although, Or, Because)
4. The baby is crying _______________ he is hungry.   (if, and, because)
5. Anand is rich _______________ greedy.   (and, so, but)
6. The bus had a flat tyre _______________ they came home walking. (so, and, but)
7. The doctor did not leave _______________ the patient stopped bleeding.
   (until, since, although)
8. You must work hard _______________ you may not get good marks. (but, and, or)
9. The kind lady gave the beggar clothes _______________ food. (because, and, so)
10. She felt lonely _______________ she adopted a baby.   (since, so, but)
11. We can eat Pizza _______________ burger.   (if, so, or)
12. She had her medicine _______________ going to bed.   (if, before, while)
13. The hare slept _______________ the tortoise reached the finishing line.
    (but, before, while)
14. Ananya went to play _______________ finishing her homework.
    (because, while, after)
15. Raju cried loudly _______________ he was hurt.   (since, when, but)
16. Red _______________ blue are both colours.   (or, and, but)
17. I'm tired _______________ I'll go to bed.   (so, if, since)
18. Turtles can swim _______________ walk.   (and, before, or)
19. The girl is happy _______________ it is her birthday.   (but, because, after)
20. Lunch is _______________ breakfast.   (after, and, or)

9 Chapter | Conjunctions

Remember

❖ Sometimes you need to revise a sentence to make sure that you have used the correct conjunction.

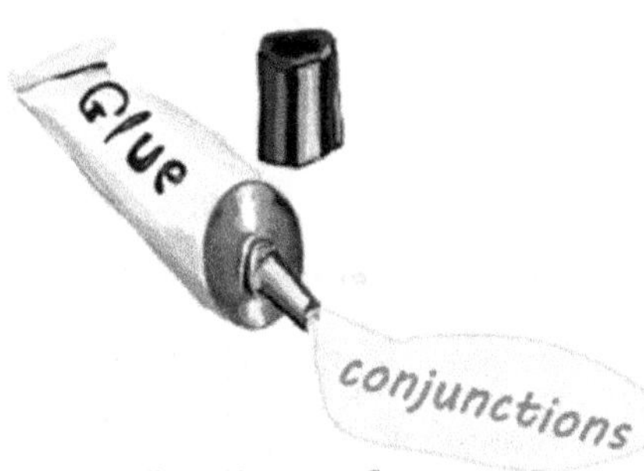

The Glue in Sentences

LEARNING OBJECTIVES

This lesson will help you to

- learn about conjunctions..
- use conjunctions to join two or more words or sentences.

INTRODUCTION

Conjunctions are also called connecting words.

We use conjunctions to join words and sentences to make them meaningful.

And, or, but, when, before, while, and after are words that are used to join sentences.

'And' is used when we want to tell more. 'And' is used when we want to express similar ideas.

For example: I can read. I can write.

I can read and write.

- **But** is used when we want to contrast the two sentences.

  For example:

  He wanted to go. He could not go. Here by adding 'but' to the two sentences we get

  Contrast; He wanted to go, but he could not go.

- **Or** is a connecting word that tells us that there is only one choice.

For example: You can go to the park. You can go to the mall.

You can go to the park.

You can go to the mall.

By adding the word 'or' we have-You can go to the park or you can go to the mall.

This makes clear that there is only one choice.

- **Because** is used when we want to give a reason for any action. The second part explains the reason for the first part. He could not attend the party because his flight **got** late.

- **When** is used to tell about two ideas occurring at the same time.

  For example: I love to go out when it's raining.

- **While** is also used to show two events happening at the same time.

  I was reading while travelling in the school bus.

- **After** is used to tell about relative time of two actions.

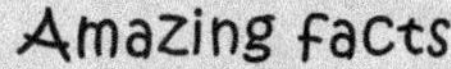

❖ There are a few conjunctions that are used as prepositions and adverbs as well.

For example: After, before, Since.

I came out of the class, after I finished my paper.

- **Before** is also used to tell about relative timing of two events.

  For example: Before I could balance myself, I fell.

Multiple Choice Questions

LEVEL - 1

Directions (Qs. 1–10): Read the following sentences and fill in the blanks from the options given below

1. I wanted to come _______ my mom did not allow me.
   - (a) and
   - (b) because
   - (c) but
   - (d) so

2. He learnt driving _______ he was in France. **(2014)**
   - (a) but
   - (b) because
   - (c) since
   - (d) while

3. The teacher punished him_____he was talking in the class.
   - (a) so
   - (b) but
   - (c) because
   - (d) as

4. I work in a bank ____ a manager.
   - (a) but
   - (b) as
   - (c) so
   - (d) because

5. The children started playing _______ the teacher had gone out. **(2015)**
   - (a) as
   - (b) since
   - (c) and
   - (d) or

6. You better finish your work _______ you will be late.
   - (a) as
   - (b) but
   - (c) since
   - (d) or

7. Debu could have gone _______ he is not well. **(2013)**
   - (a) but
   - (b) as
   - (c) since
   - (d) or

8. Get some sweets _____ coffee for me. **(2012)**
   - (a) or
   - (b) and
   - (c) but
   - (d) as

9. Though this is not my work ______, I will do it for you.
   - (a) as
   - (b) because
   - (c) and
   - (d) None of these

10. I want you to look after my child, ______ I attend my office. **(2016)**
    - (a) as
    - (b) but
    - (c) because
    - (d) while

Directions (Qs. 11–15) : Choose the conjunction from the options given below

11. (a) From   (b) Farther   **(2017)**
    (c) Frame   (d) For

12. (a) Or   (b) On   **(2013)**
    (c) An   (d) Atmost

13. (a) Not   (b) Nor   (c) No   (d) Nothing

14. (a) A   (b) An   (c) On   (d) And

15. (a) Yet   (b) But   **(2015)**
    (c) Both (a) and (b)   (d) Rain

Directions (Qs. 16–20) : Tick the pair that goes together.

16. (a) Night or day   (b) Night but day   **(2013)**
    (c) Night and day   (d) Night for day

17. (a) Tea or coffee   (b) Tea but coffee   (c) Tea yet coffee   (d) Tea so coffee

18. (a) In yet out   (b) In and out   **(2015)**
    (c) In for out   (d) In so out

19. (a) Bread and butter   (b) Bread so butter   (c) Bread if butter   (d) Bread yet butter
20. (a) Pen and paper   (b) Pen so paper   **(2014)**
     (c) Pen but paper   (d) Pen for paper
21. I ordered a cofee _______ a sandwich for lunch.
     (a) or   (b) but
     (c) so   (d) and
22. Bella is beautiful _______ arrogant.   **(2020)**
     (a) because   (b) or
     (c) if   (d) but
23. I ate ice cream _______ it was very hot today.   **(2022)**
     (a) but   (b) so
     (c) because   (d) or

LEVEL – 2

Directions (Qs. 1-15): Read the passage given below and fill in the blanks choosing the answers from the options given below.   **[Critical Thinking, 2012]**

Rahul did not like to go to school, (1) _____ he liked to play with his friends. He always tried to find an excuse to not to go to school (2) _____ he never succeeded. One day (3) _____ getting ready for school, he said he was not well. His mother got worried (4) _____ she wanted to know what had gone wrong. She did not send Rahul to school that day. The whole day Rahul kept lying on the bed. His mother wanted to know the problem. (5) _____ Rahul could not explain, this really worried his mom. (6) _____ she called up the doctor to visit him. The doctor came (7) _____ saw Rahul in the evening. The doctor could not diagnose the problem. This worried Rahul's mother more. She kept asking Rahul how he was feeling (8) _____ he did not say anything. At 6;30, in the evening, suddenly Rahul got up (9) _____ said that he was feeling better (10) _____ was going out to play. The moment Rahul said that his mother realised the problem. She came to know that(11) _____ he did not want to go to school (12) _____ he made this excuse. She was very angry. That day she did not allow him to play (13), _____ he had lied, he had to face the punishment (14) _____ she would call up his dad to tell him about today's incident. Rahul was very scared, (15) _____ he apologised to his mom. He promised his mom that he would never do this again.

1. (a) while   (b) as   (c) by   (d) but

2. (a) but   (b) while   (c) since   (d) before

3. (a) but   (b) because   (c) while   (d) as

4. (a) but   (b) while   (c) and   (d) after

5. (a) But   (b) As   (c) If   (d) So

6. (a) and   (b) but   (c) as   (d) so

7. (a) so   (b) as   (c) and   (d) or

8. (a) because   (b) and   (c) but   (d) as

9.   (a) and   (b) so   (c) but   (d) while

10. (a) since   (b) and   (c) so   (d) if

11. (a) and   (b) so   (c) as   (d) because

12. (a) so   (b) before   (c) since   (d) None of these

13. (a) as   (b) while   (c) when   (d) So

14. (a) but   (b) because   (c) If   (d) None of these

15. (a) and   (b) so   (c) before   (d) since

Directions (Qs. 16): Look at the grid given below and tell the number of conjunctions from the options given below   **[Critical Thinking]**

16.

w	a	k	g	s	l
h	f	m	k	o	b
i	t	k	j	k	h
l	e	l	m	m	v
e	r	w	h	e	n
e	n	i	f	k	m
s	i	n	c	e	n
n	j	i	h	h	l

  (a) 9   (b) 6   (c) 8   (d) 4

Directions (Qs. 17–25): Read the following sentences and identify the conjunctions. Choose the answers from the options given below.

17. She was late for the meeting because she got stuck in the traffic jam.

  (a) late   (b) meeting   (c) because   (d) traffic

18. She was doing her homework, while the teacher was teaching in the class.

  (a) doing   (b) while   (c) teacher   (d) class

19. I will go to my friend's house after the music class   **[Tricky]**

  (a) after   (b) friend's   (c) house   (d) class

20. If you don't come with me, I will not go.   (2013)

  (a) if   (b) you   (c) don't   (d) also

21. I feel happy when I go out with my family.

  (a) feel   (b) when   (c) family   (d) happy

22. I am very busy today, so I will not come for the party.   (2015)

  (a) busy   (b) today   (c) so   (d) come

23. **When I stopped him from going there, he got angry.**   (2014)

    (a)   when   (b)   told   (c)   there   (d)   angry

24. **They got scared after it got dark.**

    (a)   they   (b)   scared   (c)   after   (d)   getting

25. **Sam and Peter don't like to play cricket**   (2012)

    (a)   don't   (b)   and   (c)   like   (d)   play

Directions (Qs. 26–30): Join the following sentences using the correct conjunction. Choose the answers from the options given below.

26. **We must brush our teeth _____ going to bed.**   (2013)

    (a)   after   (b)   before   (c)   as   (d)   while

27. **It is difficult for Mac to write ______ he has hurt his finger.**

    (a)   if   (b)   as   (c)   so   (d)   after

28. **I wear sports shoes ______ I go to play.**   (2016)

    (a)   when   (b)   so   (c)   as   (d)   if

29. **You can play _____ you finish your homework.**

    (a)   as   (b)   if   (c)   so   (d)   after

30. **______ I could stop him, he went away.**   (2012)

    (a)   Before   (b)   After   (c)   As   (d)   If

Directions (Qs. 31–35) : Choose the correct option to complete the sentence.

31. You can pass if __________.

    (a)   you sleep all day   (b)   you play everyday

    (c)   you work hard   (d)   you don't study

32. It's nice and __________.

    (a)   bright in this room   (b)   boring in the room

    (c)   green in this room   (d)   gloomy here

33. We can go by car __________.

    (a)   but walk   (b)   or by bus   (c)   yet cry   (d)   so by bus

34. She wrote the exam although __________.   (2014)

    (a)   she prepared   (b)   went for a picnic

    (c)   she wanted to   (d)   she was ill

35. He sells mangoes and __________.

    (a)   rain   (b)   from   (c)   oranges   (d)   but

36. **I like to walk ______ think about things by myself.**   (2018)

    (a) nor   (b) and   (c) but   (d) so confidential

37. **I always have a shower ________ brush my teeth in the morning.**   (2019)

    (a) so   (b) or   (c) either   (d) and

RESPONSE GRID

LEVEL 1

1. a b c d   2. a b c d   3. a b c d   4. a b c d   5. a b c d
6. a b c d   7. a b c d   8. a b c d   9. a b c d   10. a b c d
11. a b c d   12. a b c d   13. a b c d   14. a b c d   15. a b c d
16. a b c d   17. a b c d   18. a b c d   19. a b c d   20. a b c d
21. a b c d   22. a b c d   23. a b c d

LEVEL 2

1. a b c d   2. a b c d   3. a b c d   4. a b c d   5. a b c d
6. a b c d   7. a b c d   8. a b c d   9. a b c d   10. a b c d
11. a b c d   12. a b c d   13. a b c d   14. a b c d   15. a b c d
16. a b c d   17. a b c d   18. a b c d   19. a b c d   20. a b c d
21. a b c d   22. a b c d   23. a b c d   24. a b c d   25. a b c d
26. a b c d   27. a b c d   28. a b c d   29. a b c d   30. a b c d
31. a b c d   32. a b c d   33. a b c d   34. a b c d   35. a b c d
36. a b c d   37. a b c d

Solutions with Explanation

LEVEL – 1

1. (c) I wanted to come but my mom did not allow me.
2. (d) He learnt driving while he was in France.
3. (c) The teacher punished him because he was talking in the class.
4. (b) I work in a bank as a manager.
5. (b) The children started playing since the teacher had gone out.
6. (d) You better finish your work or you will be late
7. (a) Debu could have gone but he is not well.
8. (b) Get some sweets and coffee for me.

9.   **(d)**   Though this is not my work, I will do it for you. (Though is a conjunction)

10. **(d)**   I want you to look after my child while I attend my office.

11. **(d)**   For   12. **(a)**   Or

13. **(b)**   Nor   14. **(d)**   And

15. **(c)**   Both (a) and (b)   16. **(c)**   Night and day

17. **(a)**   Tea or coffee   18. **(b)**   In and out

19. **(a)**   Bread and butter   20. **(a)**   Pen and paper

21. **(d)**   I ordered a coffee and a sandwich for lunch.

22. **(d)**   but

23. **(c)**   Because, it is used here to give reason.

LEVEL – 2

1.   **(d)**   but   2.   **(a)**   but
3.   **(c)**   while   4.   **(c)**   and
5.   **(a)**   But   6.   **(d)**   so
7.   **(c)**   and   8.   **(c)**   but
9.   **(a)**   and   10. **(b)**   and
11. **(d)**   because   12. **(d)**   None of these
13. **(a)**   as   14. **(d)**   None of these
15. **(b)**   so   16. **(b)**   6. while, since, when, after, if, so
17. **(c)**   because   18. **(b)**   while
19. **(a)**   after   20. **(a)**   If
21. **(b)**   when   22. **(c)**   so
23. **(a)**   When   24. **(c)**   after
25. **(b)**   and

26. **(b)**   We must brush our teeth before going to bed.

27. **(b)**   It is difficult for Mac to write as he has hurt his finger.

28. **(a)**   I wear sports shoes when I go to play.

29. **(d)**   You can play after you finish your homework..

30. **(a)**   Before I could stop him, he went away.

31. **(c)**   you work hard.

32. **(a)**   bright in this room

33. **(b)**   or by bus

34. **(d)**   she was ill

35. **(c)**   oranges

36. **(b)**   and

37. **(d)**   and

<table><tr><td>**10**</td><td></td></tr></table>

10 CHAPTER FOREWORD

Kids! In this chapter, you will learn about 'contractions'. These are two or more words put together. In contractions, an apostrophe is used for the word that has been dropped.

Can you write contractions of the underlined words in the blanks spaces given below:

1. Boys <u>are not</u> __________ playing today.

2. I <u>do not</u> __________ like sweets.

3. She <u>does not</u> __________ sing.

4. I <u>have not</u> __________ seen him.

5. <u>You will</u> __________ not go with us.

6. <u>It is</u> __________ a red ball.

7. Raunak <u>has not</u> __________ participated.

8. She was not well, so she <u>did not</u> __________ come.

9. It <u>is not</u> __________ a good car.

10. They <u>were not</u> __________ invited to the party.

11. He <u>can not</u> __________ drive well.

12. She <u>does not</u> __________ write good poem.

13. You <u>should not</u> __________ eat junk food.

14. <u>He had</u> __________ forgotten to lock the door

15. <u>She would</u> __________ enjoy the show.

10
Chapter

Contractions

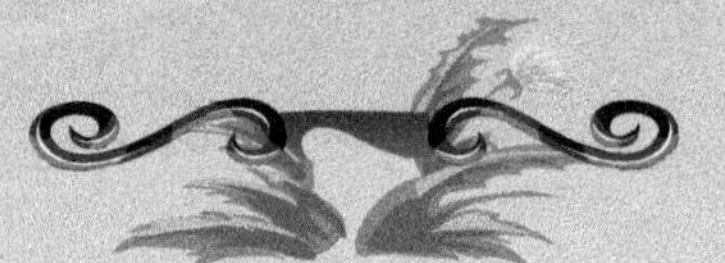

LEARNING OBJECTIVES

This lesson will help you to

* learn about contractions.
* use correct form of contractions in your writing.
* identify the contractions.

INTRODUCTION

Contractions are words that are put together to form a smaller word. But they mean the same; the meaning of the two words does not change. In contractions an apostrophe takes place of the missing letter.

For example: 'Should have' is contracted to 'should've'.

'The lion should have gone on a prowl' can also be written as

'The lion should've gone on a prowl'.

For example: I am thinking can also be written as I'm thinking.

I	I'm (I am)	I'll (I will)	I've (have)	I 'd (I had)
You	You're (you are)	You'll (you will)	You've (you have)	You'd (you had)
He	He's (he is)	He'll (he will)	He's (he has)	He'd (he had)
She	She's (she is)	She'll (she will)	She's (she has)	She'd (she had)
It	It's (it is)	It'll (it will)	It's (it has)	It'd (it had)
We	We're (we are)	We'll (we will)	We've (we have)	We'd (we had)
They	They're (they are)	They'll (they will)	They've (they have)	They'd (they had)

Negative Contractions: When two words are put together to negate something, or to say no. No is contracted to 'n't ' in the negative contractions. But the meaning does not change.

For example: 'I will not go' can also be written as 'I won't go.'

Negative contractions

Is not	Isn't
Are not	Aren't
Was not	Wasn't
Were not	Weren't
Have not	Haven't
Has not	Hasn't
Had not	Hadn't
Will not	Won't
Would not	Wouldn't
Do not	Don't
Does not	Doesn't
Did not	Didn't
Cannot	Can't
Could not	Couldn't
Should not	Shouldn't
Must not	Mustn't

I won't go

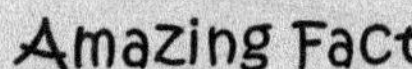

Amazing Fact

❖ Though in most of the words when they are contracted the first word remains the same but in will not, it is not contracted to will'nt the word changes to won't.

Words that ask a question are called interrogative words. **For example:** Where, how, why, who, what.

Interrogative contractions

	Is	**Will**	**Would**	**Has**	**Had**
How	How's	How'll	How'd	How's	How'd
Who	Who's	Who'll	Who'd	Who's	Who'd
What	What's	What'll	What'd	What's	What'd
Where	Where's	Where'll	Where'd	Where's	Where'd
When	When's	When'll	When'd	When's	When'd
why	Why's	Why'll	Why'd	Why's	Why'd

'Who is that?' Can also be written as 'who's that?'

Multiple Choice Questions

LEVEL – 1

Directions (Qs. 1–10): Read the following sentences and choose correct answers from the options given below

1. (a) We'ell go out today.   (b) We'el go out today.   **(2016)**
   (c) we'll go out today.   (d) We're go out today.

2. (a) Do'nt go there, its haunted.   (b) Do not go there, its haunted.
   (c) D'ont go there, its haunted.   (d) Don't go there, its haunted.

3. (a) I'am going out.   (b) I'm going out.   **(2015)**
   (c) Iam going out.   (d) I're going out.

4. (a) He'll do his work.   (b) H'll do his work.
   (c) H'ell do his work.   (d) Hel'l do his work.

5. (a) Where were you? We have been looking for you.   **(2013)**
   (b) Where were you? We've been looking for you.
   (c) Where were you? W'eve been looking for you.
   (d) Where were you? We're been looking for you.

6. (a) He should not have agreed to go.   (b) He should'nt have agreed to go.
   (c) He shouldn't have agreed to go.   (d) He doesn't have agreed to go.

7. (a) I could'nt complete my homework.
   (b) I couldn't complete my homework.
   (c) I could not complete my homework.
   (d) I 've not complete my homework.

8. (a) He has'nt been to that country.   (b) He ha'snt been to that country.
   (c) He h'snt been to that country.   (d) He hasn't been to that country.

9. (a) They do not understand English, they're from Spain.   **(2012)**
   (b) They do not understand English, theyr'e from Spain.
   (c) They do not understand English, the'yre from Spain.
   (d) They do not understand English, they are from Spain.

10. (a) There's a lot of garbage there.   (b) Ther'se a lot of garbage there.
    (c) There'se a lot of garbage there.   (d) Ther're a lot of garbage there.

Directions (Qs. 11–15) : Read the questions and choose the correct contraction from the options given.

11. He is

   (a) He's   (b) H'eis   (c) H'es   (d) Hes'

12. Who will   **(2013)**

(a) Whowi'l   (b) Who'll   (c) Who'will   (d) Whow'll

13. What would

(a) Whatwo'd   (b) Whatwou'ld   (c) What'd   (d) What'ould

14. We are   **(2012)**

(a) We're   (b) Wea'e   (c) Wear'   (d) We'are

15. You have   **(2014)**

(a) Youha'e   (b) You've   (c) You'have   (d) Y'ouhave

Directions (Qs. 16–20) : Write the word that each contraction stands for.

16. Can't

(a) Do not   (b) Could not   (c) Cannot   (d) Did not

17. Haven't   **(2016)**

(a) Has not   (b) Have not   (c) Is not   (d) Had not

18. You're   **(2017)**

(a) You are   (b) We are   (c) You have   (d) Do I

19. I'm   **(2015)**

(a) I may   (b) I am   (c) I have   (d) I will

20. You'll   **(2016)**

(a) You are   (b) You have   (c) You will   (d) You should

21. I'd done my duty.   **(2018)**

(a) I would   (b) I had   (c) I have   (d) I do

22. It's killed yesterday.   **(2019)**

(a) It is   (b) Its   (c) It was   (d) It were

LEVEL –2

Directions (Qs. 1 to 10): Read the passage carefully and replace the underlined words with their contractions from the options given below.   **(Tricky)**

Reema decided to go out with her school friends. (1) <u>They will</u> go out on sunday. (2) <u>It is</u> great fun to go for an outing with them. (3) <u>They had</u> all decided to watch a movie together. Given a choice Reema (4) <u>would not</u> have watched a movie. (5) <u>She is</u> not very fond of watching movies. But since all her friends were going (6) <u>she would</u> also go. She knew quite well that (7) <u>it will</u> be of great fun. Going out with friends is always exciting. (8) <u>They are</u> your greatest treasures. After the movie, <u>(9) they will</u> have food outside. (10) <u>It is</u> going to be a great day!

1.	(a)	They'l'l	(b)	They'll	(c)	The'yll	(d)	They'll'
2.	(a)	It's	(b)	Its'	(c)	I'ts	(d)	Its
3.	(a)	They'd	(b)	They'de	(c)	They'ed	(d)	Theyd'
4.	(a)	wouldn't	(b)	won't	(c)	would'nt	(d)	will'nt
5.	(a)	She's	(b)	She'se	(c)	She'is	(d)	She'es
6.	(a)	she'd	(b)	she'wd	(c)	she'de	(d)	she'ed
7.	(a)	itll	(b)	it'll	(c)	it'l	(d)	I'tll
8.	(a)	There're	(b)	They're	(c)	Theyr'e	(d)	Therer'e
9.	(a)	they'll	(b)	theyl'l	(c)	the'yll	(d)	theyll
10.	(a)	Its	(b)	It's	(c)	I'ts	(d)	I'ts

Directions (Qs. 11–20): Read the sentences given below and identify the contractions. Choose the answers from the options given below.

11. I won't go there, it is scary.

   (a) I   (b) won't   (c) go   (d) there

12. Shaniya would've won the race.

   (a) would've   (b) won   (c) the   (d) race

13. I'll do my homework first.

   (a) I'll   (b) do   (c) homework   (d) first

14. They aren't sure of going.   **(2013)**

   (a) They   (b) aren't   (c) sure   (d) going

15. He mustn't agree to their terms.

   (a) mustn't   (b) agree   (c) their   (d) terms

16. I wish they'd believed in me.   **(2015)**

   (a) wish   (b) they'd   (c) believed   (d) me

17. How'll she come? It is raining.   **(2014)**

   (a) How'll   (b) she   (c) come   (d) it

18. He could've driven his car.

   (a) could've   (b) his   (c) car   (d) none of these

19. Who'd clean this dirty tank?   **(2016)**

   (a) Who'd   (b) clean   (c) this   (d) dirty

20. Will he not wash the clothes?

   (a) Will   (b) he   (c) not   (d) None of these

Direction (Qs. 21): Look at the box given below and tell the number of contractions. Choose the answers from the options given below   **(Critical Thinking)**

Would	would've	should	shan't	I'll
he'll	you	you've	I	I'm

21. (a) 9   (b) 8   (c) 5   (d) 6

Directions (Qs. 22-25): Read the following passage and fill in the blanks with their contractions from the options given below.   **(Tricky, 2015)**

It __(22)__ easy for her, to buy a dress for herself. Her family was really very poor. But __(23)__ decided to buy a new dress for Christmas this year. She decided to earn money to buy it. It __(24)__ easy for a small child to earn money. She was only nine years old. How will she get money __(25)__ her concern. She could only think of a new purple dress with a bow at the waist

22. (a)   was not   (b)   wasn't   (c)   wa'snt   (d)   was'nt.

23. (a)   she'd   (b)   she'ed   (c)   she'de   (d)   shed

24. (a)   isn't   (b)   is'nt   (c)   i'snt   (d)   isnt'

25. (a)   was'nt   (b)   wasn't   (c)   wa'snt   (d)   wasn't'

Directions (Qs. 26-30) : Fill in the blanks with correct contractions in the given sentences. Choose from the given options.

26. I ________ know the reason.   **(2016)**

   (a) won't   (b) don't   (c)   haven't   (d) didn't

27. ________ gone for a picnic.

   (a) They've   (b) They're   (c)   They'll   (d) They'd

28. The kids ________ in the playground.   **(Tricky, 2015)**

   (a) shouldn't   (b) weren't   (c)   were not   (d) n't

29. ________ be gone to school.   **(2014)**

   (a) You'll   (b) You'd   (c)   You're   (d) You will

30. ________ go to the market tomorrow.   **(2017)**

   (a) Wi'l   (b) I'll   (c)   I'will   (d) I won't

RESPONSE GRID

LEVEL 1

1. a b c d   2. a b c d   3. a b c d   4. a b c d   5. a b c d

6. a b c d   7. a b c d   8. a b c d   9. a b c d   10. a b c d

11. a b c d   12. a b c d   13. a b c d   14. a b c d   15. a b c d

16. a b c d   17. a b c d   18. a b c d   19. a b c d   20. a b c d

21. a b c d   22. a b c d

LEVEL 2

1. a b c d   2. a b c d   3. a b c d   4. a b c d   5. a b c d
6. a b c d   7. a b c d   8. a b c d   9. a b c d   10. a b c d
11. a b c d   12. a b c d   13. a b c d   14. a b c d   15. a b c d
16. a b c d   17. a b c d   18. a b c d   19. a b c d   20. a b c d
21. a b c d   22. a b c d   23. a b c d   24. a b c d   25. a b c d
26. a b c d   27. a b c d   28. a b c d   29. a b c d   30. a b c d

Solutions with Explanation

LEVEL – 1

1. **(c)** We'll go out today,

2. **(d)** Don't go there, its haunted.

3. **(b)** I'm going out.

4. **(a)** He'll do his work.

5. **(b)** Where were you? We've been looking for you. .

6. **(c)** He shouldn't have agreed to go.

7. **(b)** I couldn't complete my homework.

8. **(d)** He hasn't been to that country.

9. **(a)** They do not understand English, they're from Spain.

10. **(a)** There's a lot of garbage there.

11.	**(a)**	He's	12.	**(b)**	Who'll
13.	**(c)**	What'd	14.	**(a)**	We're
15.	**(b)**	You've	16.	**(c)**	Cannot
17.	**(b)**	Have not	18.	**(a)**	You are
19.	**(b)**	I am	20.	**(c)**	You will

21. **(b)** I had

22. **(c)** It was

LEVEL - 2

1.	(b)	They'll	2.	(a)	It's
3.	(a)	they'd	4.	(a)	wouldn't
5.	(a)	She's	6.	(a)	she'd
7.	(b)	it'll	8.	(b)	They're
9.	(a)	they'll	10.	(b)	It's
11.	(b)	won't	12.	(a)	would've
13.	(a)	I'll	14.	(b)	aren't
15.	(a)	mustn't	16.	(b)	they'd
17.	(a)	how'll	18.	(a)	could've
19.	(a)	Who'd	20.	(d)	None of these
21.	(d)	6	22.	(b)	wasn't
23.	(a)	she'd	24.	(a)	isn't
25.	(b)	wasn't	26.	(b)	don't
27.	(a)	They've	28.	(b)	weren't
29.	(b)	You'd	30.	(b)	I'll

Folks! There are many punctuations marks in English language. These marks are used in a sentence to convey right meaning of the sentence. These include.,!?.

Here is an exercise based on correct use of punctuation marks.

Directions : Punctuate the following sentences.

1. happy birthday to you

   ____

2. delhi is the capital of India

   ____

3. we planted roses in the garden

   ____

4. my house is near school

   ____

5. what is your mother's name

   ____

6. daisy loves to dance

   ____

7. tom and martin are friends

   ____

8. we had fun swimming in the pool

   ____

9. angry birds in the most popular game

   ____

10. hurrrah we have won the match

   ____

<table><tr><td>

11
Chapter

</td><td>

Capitalization and Punctuation

</td></tr></table>

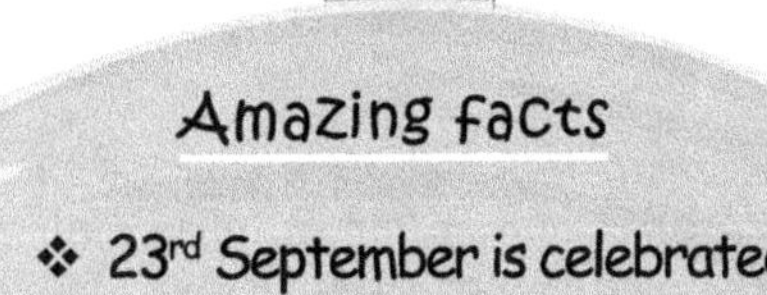

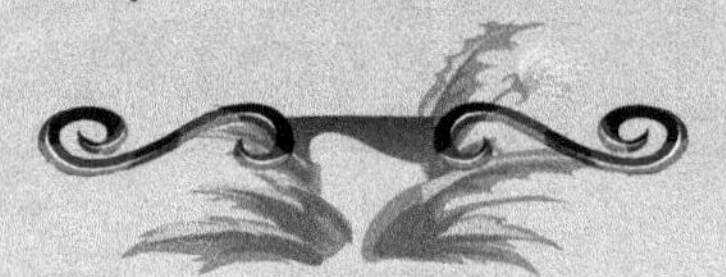

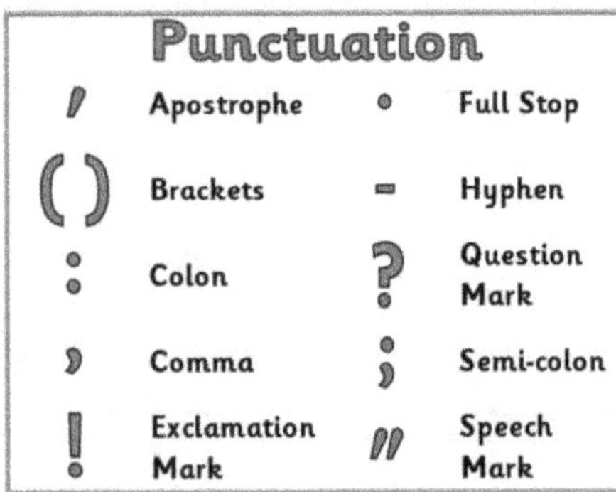

LEARNING OBJECTIVES

This lesson will help you to
- use punctuation marks.
- correctly use punctuation in English language.

INTRODUCTION

Punctuation is an important part of English language. Punctuation helps in understanding the meaning of the sentence better. Punctuation tells you whether the sentence is a question or statement. Punctuation marks can change the meaning of a sentence. If one does not use punctuation marks, the sentence would not be clear, even if one has used best of words.

For example:
- Help! A thief!

This sentence tells us that help is needed as there is a thief.
- Help a thief

This sentence asks us to help a thief, which is not correct. You did not complete your painting. It means that you are telling the other person that he or she has not completed the painting. See the other statement; did you not complete your painting? Here you seem to be questioning or interrogating the other person if he or she has completed the painting or not.

Here we would discuss the use of various punctuation marks in English.

THE USE OF CAPITAL LETTER

We use capital letter when we start any sentence. Capital letter is also used when we are using proper nouns, like

- Name of a person.
- Name of a place.
- Name of a country.
- Name of Rivers.

We also use capital letters when we write 'I' or God. I am very good at painting.

We also use capital letters in poetry. The first letter of every line is a capital letter.

For example:

> Twinke-twinke little star,
>
> How I wonder what you are?

- Inverted commas are used when we are quoting someone.

  For example: My mom said" you can't go there".

  They are used when we are directly telling about something.

- Full stops are used when we are finishing a sentence.

  For example: I went there.

  It shows that you are completing a sentence.

- Commas are used when we are talking of more than one thing and do not end the sentence.
  For example: I want to tell you that, I wasn't there. I went to the market and bought watermelon, pears, oranges and pineapple.

- Exclamation marks are used to show something unexpected or happiness.

  For example: Hurray! We won the match.

Multiple Choice Questions

LEVEL – 1

Directions (Qs. 1–10): Read the sentences given below and tell which sentence has correct punctuation. Choose the answers from the options given below.

1. (a) Where are you going?   (b) where are you going,
   (c) Where are you going.   (d) Where are you going !

2. (a) tomorrow is a holiday.   (b) Tomorrow is a holiday.
   (c) Tomorrow is a holiday?   (d) tomorrow is a Holiday !

3. (a) Mr. James is a painter by profession.   (2015)
   (b) Mr. James is a painter by profession,
   (c) Mr. james is a painter buy profession
   (d) Mr. james is a Painter by Profession.

4. (a) Tomorrow is earth day.   (b) Tomorrow is Earth Day.   (2014)
   (c) Tomorrow is earth day   (d) Tomorrow is earth Day

5. (a) today is 15th January.   (b) Today is 15th january   (2013)
   (c) today is 15th January   (d) Today is 15th January.

6. (a) cindrella is a fairy tale.   (b) Cinderella is a fairy tale
   (c) Cinderella is a Fairy tale.   (d) Cinderella is a Fairy tale

7. (a) Enid Blyton is a world famous story writer.
   (b) enid blyton is world famous story writer.
   (c) Enid blyton is world famous story writer.
   (d) enid Blyton is world famous story writer.

8. (a) i was about nine years old said Rupa.   (2012)
   (b) "i was about nine years old said rupa.
   (c) "I was about nine years old" said rupa.
   (d) "I was about nine years old" said Rupa.

9. (a) what will you write in your test.
   (b) what will you write in your test?
   (c) What will you write in your test!
   (d) What will you write in your test?

10. (a) India got independence on 15th August 1947.   (2014)
    (b) india got independence on 15th august 1947.
    (c) india got Independence on 15th august 1947.
    (d) India got independence on 15th August 1947!

Directions (Qs. 11-13) : Look at the pictures and select the correctly written word.

11. (2015)

(a) ABDUL Kalam   (b) Abdul KALAM   (c) abdul kalam   (d) Abdul Kalam

12. (2016)

(a) INDIA'S MAP   (b) India's Map   (c) India's map   (d) india's Map

13.

(a) a Police man   (b) A Policeman   (c) A POLICEMAN   (d) a Police Man

Directions (Qs. 14-18) : Choose the correct word to fill in the blanks.

14. __________ are like a father figure for me. (2012)

(a) you   (b) You   (c) YoU   (d) None of these

15. __________ is the capital of India.

(a) delhi   (b) DELHI   (c) Delhi   (d) All of these

16. The __________ is a holy river. (2016)

(a) ganges   (b) Ganges   (c) GANGES   (d) GanGes

17. __________ was built by Shah Jahan. (2015)

(a) Taj Mahal   (b) taj Mahal   (c) Taj mahal   (d) tajmahal

18. __________ is my best friend. (2014)

(a) sam   (b) SaM   (c) SAM   (d) Sam

19. **Use the correct punctuation in the given sentence.**

    Can you help me   (2019)

    (a) Full stop (.)   (b) Question mark (?)

    (c) Exclamatory mark (!)   (d) Comma (,)

20. **Rewrite the following sentence using capital and small letters at the correct places.**
                                                                     (2022)

    varanasi is a holy place in india.
    (a) varanasi is a Holy Place in india.
    (b) Varanasi is a holy place in india.
    (c) varanasi is a holy place in India.
    (d) Varanasi is a holy place in India.

LEVEL – 2

Directions (Qs. 1–10): Read the following passage carefully and fill in the blanks with the correct punctuation marks. Choose the answers from the options given below. **[Tricky]**

Doing little work at home is good for children __(1) All the children should do some work at home __(2) Even if children do little work like, keeping their toys after playing __(3) it can be of great help to parents __(4) Children become responsible if they start doing little work at home __(5) It is important that children become responsible __(6) They can do little work like dress themselves and keep their clothes in place __(7) The children love to help their parents with washing the cars __(8) going for grocery shopping or may be preparing their breakfast __(9) Helping your parents can be a daily exercise too __(10).

1. (a) .   (b) ,   (c) !   (d) ?

2. (a) .   (b) ,   (c) !   (d) ?

3. (a) !   (b) ,   (c) .   (d) ?

4. (a) .   (b) ,   (c) !   (d) ?

5. (a) .   (b) ,   (c) !   (d) ?

6. (a) .   (b) ,   (c) !   (d) ?

7. (a) .   (b) ,   (c) !   (d) ?

8. (a) .   (b) ,   (c) !   (d) ?

9. (a) .   (b) ,   (c) !   (d) ?

10. (a) . (b) , (c) ! (d) ?

Directions (Qs. 11-25): Read the following sentences and fill in the blanks with the correct punctuation marks. Choose the answers from the options given below.

11. The boy _____s toy car was broken.

    (a) , (b) . (c) ! (d) '

12. Sana has a dog ____ cat and turtle as pets

    (a) , (b) . (c) ! (d) ?

13. "Where have all the children gone _____" (2016)

    (a) , (b) . (c) ? (d) !

14. No ______ he has not done his work. (2014)

    (a) , (b) . (c) ? (d) !

15. I wasn__t punished. I was just standing out.

    (a) , (b) . (c) ? (d) '

16. Watch out ____ that house is about to collapse. (2017)

    (a) , (b) . (c) ? (d) !

17. Gina brushed her teeth _____ washed her face and got ready. (2014)

    (a) , (b) . (c) ? (d) !

18. I have read this book before _____

    (a) , (b) . (c) ? (d) !

19. Look! What is happening there _____ (2015)

    (a) , (b) . (c) ? (d) !

20. They all shouted to that lady __ asking her to stop.

    (a) , (b) . (c) ? (d) !

21. What do you want to become, when you grow up _____ (2012)

    (a) . (b) , (c) ! (d) ?

22. Hurray _____ We won the race.

    (a) . (b) , (c) ! (d) ?

23. Oops _____ We missed the bus. (2013)

    (a) . (b) , (c) ! (d) ?

24. Wow _____ That's a great news.

    (a) . (b) , (c) ! (d) ?

25. I have been to America __ France and Spain (2013)

    (a) . (b) , (c) ! (d) ?

Directions (Qs. 26–30) : Read the questions and choose the correct option.

26. We use capital letters to   (Tricky)

    (a) start a sentence   (b) write proper nouns

    (c) both (a) and (b)   (d) None of these

27. Inverted commas are used when we are   (2017)

    (a) quoting someone   (b) talking

    (c) speaking on phone   (d) to start a list

28. Which of the following is not used to end a sentence?   (2015)

    (a) .   (b) !   (c) ?   (d) ,

29. We use _____ when we are talking of more than one thing.

    (a) .   (b) ,   (c) "   (d) !

30. Every question ends with a   (2012)

    (a) fullstop   (b) exclamatory mark

    (c) question mark   (d) comma

31. How many words should be capitalized in the given sentence?   (2018)

    mumbai is the capital of maharashtra.

    (a) One   (b) Two   (c) Three   (d) Four

RESPONSE GRID

LEVEL 1

1. a b c d	2. a b c d	3. a b c d	4. a b c d	5. a b c d
6. a b c d	7. a b c d	8. a b c d	9. a b c d	10. a b c d
11. a b c d	12. a b c d	13. a b c d	14. a b c d	15. a b c d
16. a b c d	17. a b c d	18. a b c d	19. a b c d	20. a b c d

LEVEL 2

1. a b c d	2. a b c d	3. a b c d	4. a b c d	5. a b c d
6. a b c d	7. a b c d	8. a b c d	9. a b c d	10. a b c d
11. a b c d	12. a b c d	13. a b c d	14. a b c d	15. a b c d
16. a b c d	17. a b c d	18. a b c d	19. a b c d	20. a b c d

21. a b c d   22. a b c d   23. a b c d   24. a b c d   25. a b c d

26. a b c d   27. a b c d   28. a b c d   29. a b c d   30. a b c d

31. a b c d

Solutions with Explanation

LEVEL - 1

1. **(a)** Where are you going?

2. **(b)** Tomorrow is a holiday.

3. **(a)** Mr. James is a painter by profession .

4. **(b)** Tomorrow is the Earth Day.

5. **(d)** Today is 15th January

6. **(b)** Cindrella is a fairy tale.

7. **(a)** Enid Blyton is a world famous story writer.

8. **(d)** "I was about nine years old" said Rupa.

9. **(d)** What will you write in your test?

10. **(a)** India got independence on 15th August 1947.

11. **(d)** Abdul Kalam

12. **(c)** India's map

13. **(b)** A Policeman

14. **(b)** You

15. **(c)** Delhi

16. **(b)** Ganges

17. **(a)** Taj Mahal

18. **(d)** Sam

19. **(b)** Question mark (?)

20. **(d)**

LEVEL - 2

1. **(a)** .

2. **(a)** .

3. **(b)** ,

4. **(a)** .

5. **(a)** .

6. **(a)** .

7. (a) .
8. (b) ,
9. (a) .
10. (a) .
11. (d) The boy's toy car was broken.
12. (a) Sana has a dog, cat and turtle as pets.
13. (c) "Where have all the children gone"?
14. (a) No, he has not done his work.
15. (d) I wasn't punished. I was just standing out.
16. (d) Watch out! that house is about to collapse.
17. (a) Gina brushed her teeth, washed her face and got ready.
18. (b) I have read this book before.
19. (d) Look! What is happening there !
20. (a) They all shouted to that lady, asking her to stop.
21. (d) What do you want to become, when you grow up?
22. (c) Hurray! We won the race.
23. (c) Oops! We missed the bus.
24. (c) Wow! That's a great news.
25. (b) I have been to America, France and Spain.
26. (c) Both (a) and (b).
27. (a) quoting someone.
28. (d) ,
29. (b) ,
30. (c) question mark
31. (b) Two

<table><tr><td>12</td><td>

CHAPTER FOREWORD

</td></tr></table>

Kids! Your language skills are determined by the number of words that you know. 'Word Power' refers to meaning as well as usage of words.

In this chapter, you will know about words and their meanings, you will also know about words having same meanings, and words having opposite meaning.

Here is an interesting exercise for you.

Directions : Read the questions given below and choose the correct option as per the context.

1. You are happy when :

   (i) you get good marks
   (ii) you go on a picnic
   (iii) you go on a holiday
   (iv) your mother/father is with you

2. You are sad when :

   (i) you get low marks
   (ii) you fall ill
   (iii) you are hungry
   (iv) you cannot play

3. You are nervous when :

   (i) the doctor gives you an injection
   (ii) you have an exam
   (iii) you get a call from the Principal's room
   (iv) your mother/father gets angry

4. You are excited when :

   (i) you watch a good movie
   (ii) India wins a match
   (iii) you come first in class
   (iv) you play a video game

5. You are upset when :

   (i) your friend knocks you down
   (ii) your parents get angry with you
   (iii) your siblings fight with you
   (iv) your dog runs away

6. You are filled with wonder when :

   (i) your baby brother smiled at you
   (ii) you see a UFO in the sky
   (iii) the sun rises in the morning
   (iv) your pet dog plays football with you

Word Power

12

Chapter

SYNONYMS, ANTONYMS, HOMOPHONES, RHYMING WORDS COLLOCATIONS AND IDIOMS.

LEARNING OBJECTIVES

This lesson will help you to

- increase your vocabulary.
- learn spellings

INTRODUCTION

Any language needs words to express it. The words that are used should be correct enough to be understood by the other person. If you use wrong words for your expression then other person might not understand.

For example: If you say–I was very sad to see you. Whereas what you wanted to say was that you were very glad to see that person. But the wrong usage of one word may put you into trouble!

Here we will deal with Synonyms, antonyms, homophones, rhyming words collocations and idioms to enrich our understanding of English.

Synonyms are words that have similar meanings.

For example: 'Happy' can be used in place of glad.

Happy, glad

Poor, destitute

Happy	Glad
Big	Huge/enormous
Blank	Empty

Centre	Middle
Dangerous	Risky
False	Untrue
Gay	Cheerful
Hard	Difficult/ tough
High	Tall
Huge	Big
Intelligent	Clever/wise
Little	Small
Loving	Fond
Mad	Crazy
Nice	Kind
Poor	Destitute
Rich	Wealthy
Safe	Secure
Slim	Slender
Thin	lean

Sad

Happy

Antonyms are words that have opposite meanings.

For example: 'Happy' is the opposite of sad. They denote different feelings altogether.

absent	Present
Alive	Dead
Against	For
Enemy	Friend
Good	Bad
Before	After
Beautiful	Ugly

Best	Worst
Boy	Girl
Cold	Hot
Down	Up
Come	Go
Few	Many
Foolish	Wise
High	Low
Increase	Decrease
Left	Right
Less	More
Melt	Freeze
Odd	even

Homophones are words that sound similar but have different spellings.

For example: Bear, Bare. Both sound similar but have different meanings. Bear is an animal whereas Bare means to be without clothes.

Mail

Male

Hair

Hare

ad	Add
blew	Blue
Bear	Bare
By	Bye/buy
days	daze
Flee	Flea
Read	Red
Write	Right
made	Maid
Peace	Piece
Pail	Pale
One	Won
Reign	Rain
Very	Vary
Sell	Cell

Rhyming words are words that rhyme together.

For example: Tough, cough, say, may. It, sit, hit, fit, pit

Collocations are words that are put together, in a manner that they sound to be usual to a listener and the user. To be a fluent speaker in English we must know what words go together.

Have a bath
Have a drink
Have a haircut
Make a mess
Make an effort
Make room
Make trouble
Make a difference
Do me a favour
Do your best
Break a leg
Break a record
Break a promise
Break the ice
Break the news
Break the rules
Keep the promise
Keep the change
Keep in touch
Keep calm

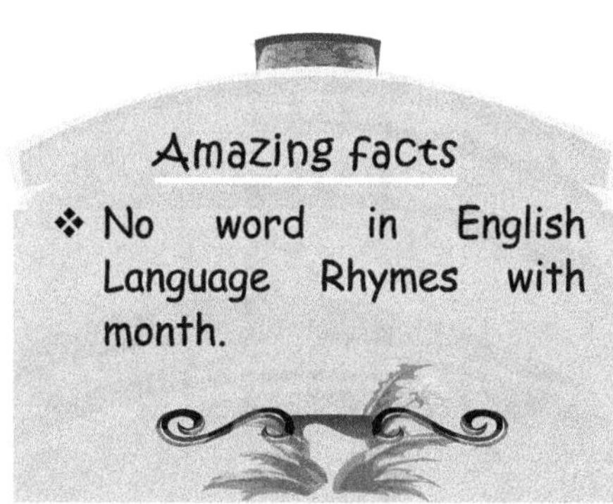

Any language has its own set of popular and wise sayings. They give us an idea of their culture and traditions. They are known as **proverbs** if they are long and **idioms** if they are short. They suggest us the ways of living and conduct in daily life.

Some popular Idioms

At the drop of a hat	Without any hesitation
Ball is in your court	It is up to you to take next decision
Best of both the worlds	All the advantages
Burn the midnight oil	To work very hard
Cut corners	Save money
Miss the boat	Miss the chance
Once in a blue moon	Happens very rarely
Piece of cake	A job that's easy or simple
See eye to eye	That two agree on something
Every cloud has a silver lining	Optimistic actions
Blessing in disguise	Something good that hasn't been recognised first.
Beat around the bush	Avoiding the main topic
Hot potato	A controversial issue on situation
Cry over spilled milk	To complain about some loss
Kill two birds with one stone	To accomplish two tasks at the same time

Multiple Choice Questions

LEVEL – 1

Directions (Qs. 1–5): Read the following sentences and replace the underlined words with their synonyms from the options given below

1. I was too <u>happy</u> to see my Dad come early from work. (2017)
   (a) sad (b) glad (c) dull (d) honest

2. His Mom got <u>furious</u> when she came to know of his low score.
   (a) happy (b) angry (c) sad (d) kind

3. Deep is very <u>polite</u> he cannot talk like that. (2016)
   (a) obedient (b) kind (c) happy (d) courteous

4. He has left most of the paper <u>blank</u>.
   (a) covered (b) empty (c) full (d) fill

5. This is such a <u>beautiful</u> house. I want to own it. (2013)
   (a) ugly (b) evil (c) awful (d) pretty.

Directions (Qs. 6–10): Read the sentences given below and replace the underlined words with their antonyms from the options given below

6. He went very <u>far</u> to see the insect. (2011)
   (a) near (b) great (c) big (d) further

7. His shirt was so <u>short</u> that he could not wear it.
   (a) wide (b) long (c) tall (d) strong

8. He was so <u>sad</u>, because he did not get a bicycle on his birthday.
   (a) nice (b) happy (c) like (d) big

9. He was too <u>weak</u> to beat him up in a fight. (2012)
   (a) weak (b) small (c) strong (d) hot

10. You forgot to give him <u>hot</u> milk along with the medicine.
    (a) hotter (b) cold (c) warm (d) frozen

Directions (Qs. 11–15): Read the following sentences and fill in the blanks with the correct word.

11. Can you buy some ______ from that shop?
    (a) flowers (b) flar (c) flawer (d) flour

12. I wanted him to come ____ to play the game. (2015)
    (a) hear (b) hair (c) here (d) hare

13. Please, can you give me your ____. I want to come to your house.
    (a) address (b) eddress (c) adress (d) udress

14. Lot of people ____ for their rights. (2013)
    (a) dye (b) die (c) dei (d) dey

15. The Sun's ___ lighten up everything.

    (a) rays   (b) raise   (c) raze   (d) rage

Directions (Qs. 16–20): Read the following sentences and fill in the blanks with their correct collocations. Choose the answers from the options given below

16. I asked my brother to "do me _________".

    (a) a favour   (b) a cooking   (c) a housework   (d) washing

17. We must make _____ to complete it.   (2016)

    (a) a difference   (b) an effort   (c) a room   (d) trouble

18. We should have ______ for the downtrodden.

    (a) a haircut   (b) sympathy   (c) a lunch   (d) a problem

19. Who will break the _____ between the both of you?   (2015)

    (a) ice   (b) rules   (c) news   (d) a record

20. Sara can you please keep___. You are making a lot of noise.   (2017)

    (a) change   (b) promise   (c) quiet   (d) in touch

Directions (Qs. 21–25): Choose the odd one out.

21. Rat, Mouse, Squirrel, Mongoose, Moon

    (a) Mouse   (b) Moon   (c) Squirrel   (d) Rat

22. Sun, Star, Moon, Waves, Galaxy   (2012)

    (a) Moon   (b) Galaxy   (c) Waves   (d) Star

23. Cinema, Theatre, Stage, Pool, Hall

    (a) Pool   (b) Theatre   (c) Cinema   (d) Hall

24. Sparrow, Dog, Parrot, Pigeon, Nightingale   (2014)

    (a) Parrot   (b) Nightingale (c) Pigeon   (d) Dog

25. Marigold, Rose, Lemon, Lotus, Jasmine

    (a) Rose   (b) Lemon   (c) Jasmine   (d) Lotus

Directions (Qs. 26–30): Choose the opposite of the given word.

26. Angry   (2016)

    (a) Honest   (b) Calm   (c) Afraid   (d) Happy

27. Cry

    (a) Scream   (b) Shout   (c) Laugh   (d) Sad

28. Hate

    (a) Like   (b) Beat   (c) Love   (d) Fight

29. Rude   (2013)

    (a) Polite   (b) Angry   (c) Clever   (d) Smart

30. **Ugly**

    (a) Intelligent (b) Honest (c) Brave (d) Beautiful

31. **Choose the synonym of upset.** (2018)

    (a) Created (b) Change (c) Disturbed (d) Develop

32. **Choose the antonym of crawl.** (2018)

    (a) Run (b) Creep (c) Surrender (d) Hide

33. **Choose the word with correct spelling.** (2018)

    (a) Reluctant (b) Creultnat (c) Luctanter (d) Trentacrul

    For questions 33 and 35, choose the word which is spelled correctly.

    Example:

    (a) Acek **(b) Cake** (c) Kace (d) Caek

34. __________ (2019)

    (a) BILNSESE (b) SENSIBLE (c) SENSEBLE (d) SENSEBIL

35. __________ (2019)

    (a) CARTUINS (b) SRCUTAIN (c) CRUTIANS (d) CURTAINS

36. **Choose the synonym of peaceful.** (2019)

    (a) Heavy (b) Evolved (c) Calm (d) Playful

37. **Choose the antonym of tired.** (2019)

    (a) Draft (b) Lively (c) Broken (d) Satisfied

38. **Choose the SYNONYM OF CONCEAL.** (2020)
    (a) Reveal (b) Hide
    (c) Expose (d) Disclose

Directions (Q. No. 39): Choose the word which is spelled correctly.

Example
    (a) Acek (b) Cake

    (b) Kace (d) Caek

39. (2021)
    (a) Maners (b) Manners
    (c) Mannars (d) Munnres

40. Choose the synonym of discard. (2021)

    (a) Agree   (b) Remove

    (c) Denote   (d) Danger

41. Choose the antonym of scold. (2021)

    (a) Scream   (b) Yell

    (c) Approve   (d) Upset

42. What is the feminine gender of drone? (2021)

    (a) Doe   (b) Queen

    (c) Sow   (d) Vixen

43. Which of these cannot be broken into pieces? (2021)

    (a) Wood   (b) Glass

    (c) Rock   (d) Sky

44. Choose the SYNONYM of frightened. (2022)

    (a) Scared   (b) comfort

    (c) Bold   (d) Glad

45. Choose the ANTONYM of accept. (2022)

    (a) Advise   (b) Reject

    (c) Burden   (d) Quite

Directions (Q. No. 46 and 47): Choose the correct answer.

46. What is the day before today called? (2022)

    (a) Date   (b) Yesterday

    (c) Week   (d) Tomorrow

47. What do you call a person who makes things from wood? (2022)

    (a) Driver   (b) Jeweller

    (c) Painter   (d) Carpenter

48. Which one of the following words rhymes with FINE? (2022)

    (a) Right   (b) Wine

    (c) Main   (d) Seen

49. Fill in the blank with the correct option as per the given hint. (2022)

Wolf . ________

    (a) Wolf   (b) Wolfs

    (c) Wolves   (d) None of these

50. Find the same meaning (Synonym) of AIM. (2022)

    (a) Directionless   (b) Neglect

    (c) Both (A) and (B)   (d) Target

51. Find the opposite meaning (Antonym) of PERIL. (2022)

    (a) Risk   (b) Careless

    (c) Lazy   (d) Safety

LEVEL – 2

Directions (Qs. 1–5): Read the passage given below and replace the underlined words with their synonyms. [Tricky]

We all like to have a (1) <u>big</u> amount of money. Who does not (2) <u>like</u> money?

Money is like a magnet that attracts a lot of people to you. Even if you have a (3) <u>little</u> money, you want to buy a lot of things. Once you have money in your pocket, you can have some of your (4) <u>wishes</u> come true. But only money cannot make you (5) <u>happy</u>.

1.	(a) small	(b) big	(c) huge	(d) little
2.	(a) love	(b) hate	(c) dislike	(d) big
3.	(a) small	(b) big	(c) huge	(d) kind
4.	(a) true	(b) false	(c) kind	(d) hope
5.	(a) kind	(b) glad	(c) sad	(d) unhappy.

Directions (Qs. 6–10): Read the following passage and replace the underlined words with their antonyms. Choose the answers from the options given below.

[Tricky, 2015]

Have you seen an ant? It is such a (6) <u>big</u> animal. It is known for its storing capacity. One day an ant was going home after collecting its food. On its way it met a mouse. The mouse was (7) <u>smaller</u> than it. The ant (8) <u>politely</u> asked the mouse "where were you? Your mother is looking for you". The mouse replied in a (9) <u>loud</u> voice "who are you to ask me this?" The ant replied in a (10) <u>quiet</u> voice," I said your mom is looking for you, she is worried.".

6.	(a) small	(b) great	(c) big	(d) further
7.	(a) bigger	(b) hut	(c) old	(d) strong
8.	(a) sharply	(b) rudely	(c) kindly	(d) happily
9.	(a) quiet	(b) happy	(c) sad	(d) excited
10.	(a) quiet	(b) lovely	(c) loud	(d) beautiful

Directions (Qs. 11–15): In the following passage replace the underlined words with their collocations. Choose the answers from the options given below.

[Tricky]

I was already getting late for work so I decided to (11)___________taxi. I was in a hurry, I could not wait to take the money back. I told the taxi driver to (12) ________. I am always reminded of my Dad's words "Do (13)_______in everything. I do not want be late anywhere. It always (14)_______ a difference. I never (15)-_______chance when it comes to work.

11. (a) take a   (b) make a   (c) break a   (d) keep

12. (a) Keep the money   (b) Keep the change

     (c) make a change   (d) break a promise

13. (a) your best   (b) your work

     (c) your homework   (d) your cleaning

14. (a) keeps   (b) makes   (c) takes   (d) breaks

15. (a) make   (b) take   (c) break   (d) do

Directions (Qs. 16–20): Read the passage given below and fill in the blanks with a correct word from the options given below.

Yesterday, I saw a __(16) it wanted me to free it from a cage. __(17) was too scared of doing so. So I came without looking at it. __(18) passed, I did not go via that place. It was __(19) tough to avoid going there. But I would turn __(20) instead of going straight where that animal was kept in the cage. We should not keep animals in cages. We all love our freedom. Animals must also be loving it.

16. (a) hare   (b) hair   (c) here   (d) hear

17. (a) Eye   (b) I   (c) Ei   (d) Ii

18. (a) Daze   (b) Days   (c) Dais   (d) Dazes

19. (a) vary   (b) very   (c) berry   (d) veri

20. (a) right   (b) write   (c) rite   (d) wright

Directions (Qs. 21–25): Read the sentences given below and fill in the blanks completing the idioms. Choose the answers from the options given below.

21. **Now the ball is_____. You have to decide.**   **(2014)**

     (a) in your court   (b) in your pocket

     (c) in my room   (d) in the cupboard.

22. **You can't have best of ________.**   **(2016)**

     (a) nowhere   (b) both the worlds

     (c) the party   (d) the haircut

23. **He has burnt _______ to come first.**

     (a) his hands   (b) his fingers

     (c) the midnight oil.   (d) his clothes

24. **He comes here only once _______________.**

     (a) in two weeks   (b) in a blue moon

     (c) never   (d) everyday

25. **It is not a piece of a/an ________. It's going to be tough.**

     (a) pie   (b) apple   (c) cake   (d) pizza

Directions (Qs. 26–30): Read the poem given below and answer the questions from the options given below.   **[Critical Thinking, 2013]**

        I am a brat

        I love to laugh, though it is tough

        When you(26)_______,

I love to play

When you want me study whole(27) _____,

I want to cry

For games you don't even(28)_____

I love to laugh at the clown

When you all (29)____

Do you know what?

It's not easy to be a(30) _____

26. **The rhyming word for laugh here would be**

    (a) calf   (b) half   (c) cough   (d) half

27. **The rhyming word for play here would be**

    (a) day   (b) may   (c) say   (d) stay

28. **The rhyming word for cry here would be**

    (a) fry   (b) try   (c) dry   (d) my

29. **The rhyming word for clown would be**

    (a) down   (b) frown   (c) mown   (d) brown

30. **The rhyming word for what here is**

    (a) brat   (b) cat   (c) mat   (d) rat

Directions (Qs. 31–35): Choose the correct word pair:

31. **Television is to watch as radio is to _________.**   (2012)

    (a) listen   (b) see   (c) sing   (d) observe

32. **Dictionary is to words as book is to _________.**   (2013)

    (a) write   (b) erase   (c) story   (d) notebook

33. **School is to study as stadium is to _________.**

    (a) play   (b) read   (c) dance   (d) talk

34. **Sandwich is to eat as flower is to _________.**   (2014)

    (a) pluck   (b) crush   (c) eat   (d) smell

35. **Doctor is to hospital as postman is to _________.**   (2015)

    (a) school   (b) shop   (c) post office   (d) bank

36. **Choose the ANTONYM OF GENTLY.**   (2020)

    (a) Kindly   (b) Lovingly

    (c) Brutally   (d) Mildly

37. What do you call the person who is trained to travel in space? (2020)

(a) Pilot

(b) Astronaut

(c) Astrologer

(d) Driver

38. Choose the SYNONYM OF SLEEPY. (2021)

(a) Lively   (b) Heavily   (c) Sparkly   (d) Drowsy

39. Choose the SYNONYM OF ACTIVATE. (2022)

(a) Start

(b) Close

(c) Finish

(d) Imitate

40. Arrange the jumbled letters to make a meaningful wor(d) (2022)

A E R N M N

(a) Manenr

(b) Manner

(c) Mennar

(d) Mannre

41. Match the words given in column O with the words given in column P to form other meaningful words: (2022)

	O		P
i.	Play	a.	Apple
ii.	Fire	(b)	Man
iii.	Pine	(c)	Ground
iv.	Brief	(d)	Case

(a) i. → c, ii. → a, iii. → b, iv. → d

(b) i. → c, ii. → b, iii. → a, iv. → d

(c) i. → d, ii. → b, iii. → a, iv. → c

(d) i. → c, ii. → d, iii. → a, iv. → b

42. How many letters of vowels and consonants are used respectively in the spelling of the figure shown below? (2022)

(a) Five vowels and five consonants

(b) Three vowels and seven consonants

(c) Four vowels and six consonants

(d) Six vowels and seven consonants

43. Fill in the blanks with correct letters to make a meaningful word. **(2022)**
___BTAI___
(a) E, K (b) A, E
(c) A, N (d) O, N

44. Find the correct match. **(2022)**
Dog : Bitch : : Horse : ?
(a) Doe
(b) Vixen
(c) Mare
(d) Sow

RESPONSE GRID

LEVEL 1

1. a b c d 2. a b c d 3. a b c d 4. a b c d 5. a b c d
6. a b c d 7. a b c d 8. a b c d 9. a b c d 10. a b c d
11. a b c d 12. a b c d 13. a b c d 14. a b c d 15. a b c d
16. a b c d 17. a b c d 18. a b c d 19. a b c d 20. a b c d
21. a b c d 22. a b c d 23. a b c d 24. a b c d 25. a b c d
26. a b c d 27. a b c d 28. a b c d 29. a b c d 30. a b c d
31. a b c d 32. a b c d 33. a b c d 34. a b c d 35. a b c d
36. a b c d 37. a b c d 38. a b c d 39. a b c d 40. a b c d
41. a b c d 42. a b c d 43. a b c d 44. a b c d 45. a b c d
46. a b c d 47. a b c d 48. a b c d 49. a b c d 50. a b c d
51. a b c d

LEVEL 2

1. a b c d 2. a b c d 3. a b c d 4. a b c d 5. a b c d
6. a b c d 7. a b c d 8. a b c d 9. a b c d 10. a b c d
11. a b c d 12. a b c d 13. a b c d 14. a b c d 15. a b c d
16. a b c d 17. a b c d 18. a b c d 19. a b c d 20. a b c d
21. a b c d 22. a b c d 23. a b c d 24. a b c d 25. a b c d
26. a b c d 27. a b c d 28. a b c d 29. a b c d 30. a b c d

31. a b c d   32. a b c d   33. a b c d   34. a b c d   35. a b c d
36. a b c d   37. a b c d   38. a b c d   39. a b c d   40. a b c d
41. a b c d   42. a b c d   43. a b c d   44. a b c d

Solutions with Explanation

LEVEL – 1

1. **(b)** glad

2. **(b)** angry

3. **(d)** courteous

4. **(b)** empty

5. **(d)** pretty.

6. **(a)** He went very near to see the insect.

7. **(b)** His shirt was so long that he could not wear it.

8. **(b)** He was so happy, because he did not get a bicycle on his birthday.

9. **(c)** He was so strong to beat him up in a fight.

10. **(b)** You forgot to give him cold milk along with the medicine.

11. **(a)** Can you buy some flowers from that shop?

12. **(c)** I wanted him to come here to play the game.

13. **(a)** Please, can you give me your address, I want to come to your house.

14. **(b)** Lot of people die for their rights.

15. **(a)** The Sun's rays lighten up everything.

16. **(a)** I asked my brother to "do me a favour".

17. **(b)** We must make an effort to complete it.

18. **(b)** We should have sympathy for the downtrodden.

19. **(a)** Who will break the ice between the two of you?

20. **(c)** Sara can you please keep quiet. You are making a lot of noise.

21. **(b)** Moon; All others are animals

22. **(c)** Waves; All others are related to universe

23. **(a)** Pool; All others are places where plays are performed

24. **(d)** Dog; All others are birds

25. **(b)** Lemon; All others are flowers

26. **(b)** Calm

27. (c) Laugh	**28.** (c) Love	
29. (a) Polite	**30.** (d) Beautiful	

31. (c) Disturbed

32. (a) Run

33. (a) Reluctant

34. (b) SENSIBLE

35. (d) CURTAINS

36. (c) Calm

37. (b) Lively

38. (b) Hide

39. (b) Manners is the correct spelling.

40. (b) The synonym of Discard is 'remove'.

41. (c) The antonym of scold is 'approve'.

42. (b) The feminine of drone is queen.

43. (d) Sky cannot be broken into pieces.

44. (a) The word frightened means to be scared. Other word for this can be afraid.

45. (b) The antonym of accept is reject.

46. (b) The day before today is called yesterday.

47. (d) The person who makes things from wood is called a carpenter.

48. (b)

49. (c)

50. (d)

51. (d)

LEVEL – 2

1. (c) Huge	**2.** (a) Love
3. (a) Small	**4.** (d) Hopes
5. (b) Glad	**6.** (a) Small
7. (a) bigger	**8.** (b) Rudely
9. (a) Quiet	**10.** (c) Loud
11. (a) take a	**12.** (b) Keep the change
13. (a) your best	**14.** (b) makes
15. (b) take	**16.** (a) hare

17. (b) I	**18.** (b) Days
19. (b) very	**20.** (a) right

21. (a) Now the ball is in your court. You have to decide.

22. (b) You can't have best of both the worlds.

23. (c) He has burnt the midnight oil to come first.

24. (b) He comes here only once in a blue moon.

25. (c) It is not a piece of a cake. It's going to be tough.

26. (c) cough	**27.** (a) day.
28. (b) try	**29.** (b) frown
30. (a) brat	**31.** (a) listen
32. (c) story	**33.** (a) play
34. (d) smell	**35.** (c) post office

36. (b) Astronaut

37. (c) Brutally

38. (d) The synonym of sleepy is drowsy.

39. (a) Start is the synonym of activate.

40. (b)

41. (b) **42.** (c)   **43.** (d)   **44.** (c)

13 # CHAPTER FOREWORD

This chapter deals with spellings. You all will agree that knowledge of correct spelling is a basic requirement for good written English.

Before you start reading this chapter, here is an exercise for you based on spellings.

Directions : Fill in the blanks with two letters.

1. _______eep

2. _______ mon

3. _______ a cock

4. _______ eek

5. _______ ush

6. _______ tch

7. _______ ple

8. _______ use

9. _______ own

10. _______ ife

Making a Word and Identifying a Word from a Picture

Amazing Facts

Cna yuo Raed tihs?

❖ It is often said that only the first and last letter of the word should be intact and it can be read.

❖ But only 55 out of 100 people can read that way.

LEARNING OBJECTIVES

This lesson will help you to

- identify a word from looking at the picture.
- increase your vocabulary and spellings.

INTRODUCTION

In any language it is important that we use correct spellings. Otherwise the other person might not understand what we mean to say. When we use incorrect spellings the meaning of what we want to convey is not understood properly.

For example: if we say we went together for a party.

Instead of writing **together** we wrote **to gather**, it changes the meaning of the whole sentence. To gather means to get collected whereas together means to do something with someone.

For example: The crowd gathered to see the show.

We went together
for a party.

The crowd gathered
to see the show.

If words or sentences are not put in correct order then they cannot explain the correct idea.

For example: If I say, I in the park was.. Does it make any sense? No!

But when I say I was in the park it is quite clear that I was in the park

Or if we read a mouse after ran cat. What will you understand? Nothing. Lets put it the other way A cat ran after the mouse; now it's clear that a cat ran after a mouse and not a mouse ran after a cat! That can be amazing too!

Spelling of any given word is equally important. If the spellings are not correct, then the correct idea cannot be conveyed. For example: If you write tealescope instead of telescope, the reader might not understand it.

Tealescope- Does it look correct? No, it does not. The correct spelling is telescope.

Let's take another example- A Dolfin. Do you think it's the correct spelling? No, it is not. The correct spelling is Dolphin. 'ph' sounds as 'f' as in telephone.

Here instead of writing light, if we write lite, what will it mean? Nothing. The correct spelling for it is light. (ight says ite as in might, sight, fight)

Let's take another example- Ruf. Did you get an idea about what is being talked about? No!

Actually the word means something that's not smooth but coarse. When explained further we came to know that it was Rough that was being talked about. A rough seashell. (here ough) sounds as uff as in tough)

What is this? Ice or ic or is?

It's Ice. (when i-e then I is sounded as 'I' as in I)

I was in the park.

Light

Multiple Choice Questions

LEVEL - 1

Directions (Qs. 1-8): Look at the pictures and identify the correct word for them.

1. (a) Racket   (b) Rocket   (c) Raket   (d) Raquet

(2016)

2. (a) Rainbow   (b) Ranbow   (c) Rainbo   (d) Rainbou

3. (a) Lemon   (b) lamoen   (c) Lamon   (d) Leman

(2012)

4. (a) Restarent   (b) Restaurant   (c) Rastaurant   (d) Restarent

(2015)

5. (a) Nife   (b) Knife   (c) Kniph   (d) Nif

(2014)

6.   (a) Laf   (b) Laff   (c) Laugh   (d) Lough

(2015)

7.   (a) Nest   (b) Nast   (c) Nist   (d) Neast

(2013)

8.   (a) Babby   (b) Babi   (c) Baby   (d) Babbi

Directions (Qs. 9-18): Choose the correct spellings from the options given below

9.   (a) Daghter   (b) Daughter
      (c) Dauter   (d) Dughter

10.   (a) loin   (b) Lion   **(2014)**
      (c) Lyon   (d) Loyn

11.   (a) Tommorow   (b) Tommorrow   **(2013)**
      (c) Tomorrow   (d) Tommorro

12.   (a) Beautifull   (b) Butiful
      (c) Beautiful   (d) Beauteful

13.   (a) Danjres   (b) Dangerous   **(2015)**
      (c) Dangeres   (d) Danjrous

14.   (a) Medisine   (b) Medicine   **(2014)**
      (c) Madisine   (d) Madisine

15.   (a) Searvants   (b) Servents   (c) Servants   (d) Sarvants

16.   (a) Girls   (b) Gils   (c) Gril   (d) Garls

17.   (a) Realiz   (b) Relieaze   **(2012)**
      (c) Realize   (d) Rialize

18.   (a) Tyere   (b) Tired   (c) Tiree   (d) Tyred

Directions (Qs. 19-23) : Look at the picture and choose the correct option.

19. (a)   The boy is flying a kite.   (b)   They are flying a kite.   **(2012)**

    (c)   This is a kite.   (d)   Kite is dancing.

20. (a)   She is having dinner.   (b)   Me is having dinner.   **(2016)**

    (c)   We are having dinner.   (d)   Them are having dinner.

21. (a)   Seema prays every night.   (b)   Seema pray night.

    (c)   Seema prayer every night.   (d)   Seema prayers every night.

22. (a)   He is a baker.   (b)   He is a cleaner.   **(2017)**

    (c)   He is a teacher.   (d)   He is a clown.

23. (a) It is a hair dresser.　　　　(b) She is a hair dresser.

    (c) He is a hair dresser.　　　　(d) They are hair dressers.

24. **Timmy has _________ sister.**　　　　　　　　　　　**(2018)**

(a) one　　　　(b) two　　　　(c) three　　　　(d) no

25. **Walter is the _________ man.**　　　　　　　　　　　**(2018)**

(a) smallest　　　(b) richest　　　(c) oldest　　　(d) tallest

26. **Timmy has _________ hair than his cousin Alan.**　　　　**(2018)**

(a) fatter　　　(b) shorter　　　(c) brown　　　(b) sadder

27. Nancy is Alan's __________. (2018)

    (a) sister   (b) cousin   (c) mother   (d) aunty

28. Which kind of fruit is red ? (2018)

    (a) Strawberry   (b) Coconut   (c) Avocado   (d) Lemon

29. Fill in the blank with missing letters as per the given hint. (2022)

    (a) USHEO   (b) OOSHO
    (c) USHIO   (d) OSHIO

30. Fill in the blanks with correct vowels as per the picture given below. (2022)

    (a) A, O   (b) E, O
    (c) E, A   (d) A, E

LEVEL - 2

Directions (Qs. 1–5): In the following passages, notice the underlined words. Choose their correct spelling from the options given below

1. Once there was a boy named Harry. He did not like to help any <u>persun</u>. He used to look down upon anyone who asked for his help. Though he was very good at studies but when it came to helping any of his <u>classmetes</u> with their studies he refused to do so. His behaviour was such that no one made him their friend. One day while coming to school he fell in a pit. One of his classmates, whom he had turned away only a day back, saw him falling. Harry did not expect him to come forward for help. But that boy helped him to come out. This changed Harry's <u>beehaviour</u> forever. Now he became a friendly person who would <u>allways</u> come forward to help others.

    Choose correctly spelt words from the following options.   [Critical Thinking]

    1.   person
    2.   classmetes
    3.   behaviour
    4.   allways

    (a)   1 and 3   (b)   1, 2 and 3   (c)   2, 3 and 4   (d)   3 and 4

2. Last Sunday I went to a zoo with my classmates. We went by our school bus. We reached around 10 O' clock in the <u>moning</u>. We were very excited to see <u>differant</u> types of animals there. We saw a gorilla, <u>girraffe</u>, lion, tiger and lot of more animals. I wanted to feed the animals but we were told not to feed the animals because they might get <u>excitted</u>, and then attack on us for more food. We stayed there for about three hours. We reached school around 1PM.

    Choose correctly spelt words from the following options.   (2013)
    1.   moning
    2.   different
    3.   giraffe
    4.   excitted
    (a)   1 and 2   (b)   2 and 3
    (c)   3 and 4   (d)   2 and 4

3. My mom always warns me to not to open the door to <u>strongers</u>. That day also she had warned me" Do not open the door for strangers". <u>Aftar</u> she left, the <u>doorebell</u> rang, I forgot what my mother had always warned me about and opened the door. On the door was <u>stending</u> a salesman.

    1.   strongers

2.   after

3.   doorbell

4.   standing

(a) 1, 2 and 3   (b) 2, 3 and 4

(c) 1, 3 and 4   (d) 1, 2 and 4

4. Pam was <u>tyred</u> of going to the same park. His parents had <u>promesed</u> to take him to a zoo this time. Pam was really excited about it. He was waiting for the <u>weekand</u>. On Sunday morning, he got up very early. He woke up his parents. They all got ready to go. When they came out of the house, they saw that their tyre was <u>puntured</u>.   (2015)

1.   tyred

2.   weekend

3.   promesed

4.   punctured

(a) 1 and 2   (b) 2 and 4

(c) 1, 2 and 3   (d) 1, 2 and 4

5. Pushkar is my <u>cousine</u>. He comes <u>evary</u> weekend to have <u>dinnar</u> with us. We all like his company. But this weekend he did not come. So, we got worried. We tried calling him, but his number could not be reached. He did not even call us to <u>infom</u> about it.   (2016)

1.   cousin

2.   every

3.   dinner

4.   infom

(a) 1, 2 and 3   (b) 1, 2 and 4

(c) 2, 3 and 4   (d) All of the above

Directions (Qs. 6): Read the passage given below and choose the correct spelling of the underlined words from the options given below.   (Tricky, 2012)

Nethra suffers from walking ___(6) (disabiliti). She cannot ___(7) (wak) and so uses a wheelchair. She ___(8) (nos) that people look at her with sympathy, but she does not bother. She tries to lead a normal life. She goes to school, and goes to ___(9) (cinima) also. She has sister who is normal. Her sister is her best ___(10) (freind).

6.   (a) disability   (b) disebilty   (c) desiblty   (d) dasibiliti

7.   (a) wlak   (b) wkal   (c) walk   (d) walak

8.   (a) Knos   (b) Knows   (c) nows   (d) Knous

9. (a) cinama   (b) cinema   (c) cinima   (d) cenima
10. (a) frind   (b) frend   (c) friend   (d) frand

Directions (Qs. 11 to 20): Read the following sentences and fill in the blanks with the correct spellings from the options given below.

11. The birds make their nest on the _______ of the tree.
    (a) brunches   (b) branches   (c) branchs   (d) brenches

12. A ___________ is a very poisonous reptile.   **(2016)**
    (a) snake   (b) sneke   (c) snak   (d) snack

13. We wear _____ on a cold day.   **(2013)**
    (a) cot   (b) coat   (c) caot   (d) cote

14. We live in a very big _______.
    (a) house   (b) hose   (c) huose   (d) huse

15. We row a _____to cross a river.   **(2014)**
    (a) bote   (b) boat   (c) baot   (d) bot

16. He plays _______ very well.
    (a) drem   (b) drom   (c) drum   (d) dram.

17. **We went to Manali and made a _______ man.**   **(2015)**
    (a) sno   (b) snow   (c) snou   (d) snew

18. **Ganga is a big _______.**
    (a) revir   (b) river   (c) rivir   (d) rivur

19. **He poured tea into a _____.**   **(2012)**
    (a) cap   (b) cup   (c) cep   (d) cop

20. **We ate ______ for lunch.**
    (a) cake   (b) cak   (c) caka   (d) cacke

Directions (Qs. 21–30): Read the following sentences and fill in the blanks with the correct word Choose the answer from the options given below

21. **My dog likes to chew a __________.**   **(2016)**
    (a) boen   (b) bone   (c) oben   (d) nebo

22. **We must ______ at the red light.**
    (a) psto   (b) sopt   (c) stop   (d) tsop

23. **After forty nine comes ______.**
    (a) fitfy   (b) tiffy   (c) iffty   (d) fifty

24. **There are twelve months in a ______.**   **(2015)**
    (a) eayr   (b) year   (c) ayre   (d) reay

25. **Your hands are dirty, my hands are ________.**   **(2016)**
    (a) lcaen   (b) elcan   (c) clena   (d) clean

26. I bite my food with my _______. (2014)
    (a) teeth (b) theet (c) eteth (d) heett

27. I am dark, and an opposite of day. I am _______.
    (a) nghti (b) tighn (c) ightn (d) night

28. I will wear a ______ dress for the meeting tomorrow. (2017)
    (a) green (b) ngree (c) egren (d) engre.

29. Today is Shan's ninth _______. (2013)
    (a) birthday (b) daybirth (c) brithday (d) dyathrib

30. The _____ crow was looking for water everywhere. (2015)
    (a) htirsy (b) thsirty (c) thristy (d) thirsty

Directions (Qs. 31–35): Choose the correct sentence from the given options.

31. Hari / neatly / letter / the / wrote
    (a) Hari wrote the letter neatly. (b) Neatly the letter wrote Hari.
    (c) Hari neatly wrote the letter. (d) Hari wrote neatly letter the.

32. Mother / is / your / a / ? / doctor
    (a) your mother is doctor? (b) Is your mother a doctor?
    (c) your mother a is doctor? (d) Is your mother ? A doctor

33. Very / I / tired / am
    (a) I am very tired. (b) Very tired I am.
    (c) Very tired am I. (d) I very tired am.

34. Me / to / junior / is / Asha (Critical Thinking, 2016)
    (a) Me to junior is Asha. (b) Asha to me is junior.
    (c) Asha is junior to me. (d) Asha junior is to me.

35. Cut / trees / the / don't
    (a) Don't cut the trees. (b) Cut don't the trees.
    (c) The trees don't cut. (d) Don't the trees cut.

For questions 36 to 40, look at the picture and choose the correct answer.
  (2019)

Example:

There are _________ children running.

(a) lots of (b) two (c) no (d) a couple

36. The blonde girl _______ with her mother.

(a) is eating   (b) is playing   (c) is running   (d) is shouting

37. The boy on the right has ________ shorts. (2019)

(a) yellow   (b) blue   (c) black   (d) white

38. The man at the back has black _______ on. (2019)

(a) glasses   (b) gloves   (c) leggings   (b) armbands

39. The people in the race all look _______. (2019)

(a) happy   (b) sad   (c) tired   (d) thirsty

40. The race is on a ________. (2019)

(a) road   (b) stadium   (c) playground   (d) forest

Directions (Q. No. 41 to 46): Choose the correct option to fill in the blank.

(2020)

41. _________ are on the swings. (2020)

(a) Riya and Mohan

(b) Kirti and Mohan

(c) Rahul and Jatin

(d) Rahul and Mohan

> Example
>
> There are ____ children in the image
>
> (a) four   (b) five
>
> (c) six   (d) three

42. Rahul and Riya are playing in the __________.   (2020)

    (a) class   (b) sand-pit

    (c) beach   (d) play-house

43. Bonzo is sitting __________ Rahul.   (2020)

    (a) under   (b) between

    (c) beside   (d) along

44. There are two __________ in the back.   (2020)

    (a) trees   (b) men

    (c) beside   (d) along

45. __________ is wearing a cap.

    (a) Jatin   (b) Kirti

    (c) Rahul   (d) Mohan

46. Identify the picture shown below and choose the correct spelling.   (2022)

    (a) Broccolee

    (b) Brocooli

    (c) Brocoli

    (d) Broccoli

RESPONSE GRID

LEVEL 1

1. a b c d	2. a b c d	3. a b c d	4. a b c d	5. a b c d
6. a b c d	7. a b c d	8. a b c d	9. a b c d	10. a b c d
11. a b c d	12. a b c d	13. a b c d	14. a b c d	15. a b c d
16. a b c d	17. a b c d	18. a b c d	19. a b c d	20. a b c d
21. a b c d	22. a b c d	23. a b c d	24. a b c d	25. a b c d
26. a b c d	27. a b c d	28. a b c d	29. a b c d	30. a b c d

LEVEL 2

1. a b c d   2. a b c d   3. a b c d   4. a b c d   5. a b c d
6. a b c d   7. a b c d   8. a b c d   9. a b c d   10. a b c d
11. a b c d   12. a b c d   13. a b c d   14. a b c d   15. a b c d
16. a b c d   17. a b c d   18. a b c d   19. a b c d   20. a b c d
21. a b c d   22. a b c d   23. a b c d   24. a b c d   25. a b c d
26. a b c d   27. a b c d   28. a b c d   29. a b c d   30. a b c d
31. a b c d   32. a b c d   33. a b c d   34. a b c d   35. a b c d
36. a b c d   37. a b c d   38. a b c d   39. a b c d   40. a b c d
41. a b c d   42. a b c d   43. a b c d   44. a b c d   45. a b c d
46. a b c d

Solutions with Explanation

LEVEL - 1

1. (a) Racket
2. (a) Rainbow
3. (a) Lemon
4. (b) Restaurant
5. (b) Knife. The rule is that when k comes with n then k is silent.
6. (c) laugh
7. (a) Nest
8. (c) Baby
9. (b) Daughter
10. (b) Lion
11. (c) Tomorrow
12. (c) Beautiful
13. (b) Dangerous
14. (b) Medicine
15. (c) servants
16. (a) Girls
17. (c) Realize
18. (b) Tired
19. (a) The boy is flying a kite
20. (c) We are having dinner
21. (a) Seema prays every night
22. (a) He is a baker
23. (b) She is a hair dresser
24. (a) one
25. (c) oldest
26. (b) shorter
27. (d) aunty
28. (a) Strawberry
29. (c)
30. (b)

LEVEL – 2

1. **(a)** 1 and 3   2. **(b)** 2 and 3
3. **(b)** 2, 3 and 4   4. **(b)** 2 and 4
5. **(a)** 1, 2 and 3   6. **(a)** disability
7. **(c)** walk
8. **(b)** knows. (When k comes with n then k remains silent as in knife.)
9. **(b)** cinema
10. **(c)** friend
11. **(b)** The birds make their nest on the branches of the tree.
12. **(a)** A snake is a very poisonous reptile. Reptiles are living beings that lay eggs and have scales on them.
13. **(b)** We wear coat on a cold day.   14. **(a)** We live in a very big house.
15. **(b)** We row a boat to cross a river.   16. **(c)** He plays drum very well.
17. **(b)** We went to Manali and made a snow man. Manali is a hill station situated in Himachal Pradesh
18. **(b)** Ganga is a big river. Ganga is the name of a river.
19. **(b)** He poured tea into a cup.   20. **(a)** We ate cake for lunch.
21. **(b)** My dog likes to chew a bone.
22. **(c)** We must stop at the red light.
23. **(d)** After forty nine comes fifty
24. **(b)** There are twelve months in a year.
25. **(d)** Your hands are dirty, my hands are clean.
26. **(a)** I bite my food with my teeth
27. **(d)** I am dark and an opposite of day .I am night.
28. **(a)** I will wear a green dress for the meeting tomorrow.
29. **(a)** Today is Shan's ninth birthday.
30. **(d)** The thirsty crow was looking for water everywhere.
31. **(a)**   32. **(b)**   33. **(a)**
34. **(c)**   35. **(a)**
36. **(c)** is running   37. **(d)** white
38. **(c)** leggings   39. **(a)** happy
40. **(a)** road   41. **(b)** Kirti and Mohan
42. **(b)** sand-pit   43. **(c)** beside
44. **(a)** trees
45. **(d)** Mohan
46. **(d)**

14 | CHAPTER FOREWORD

You all will agree that language has an important role in our life. A command over language influences our spoken and written expression.

Here is an exercise that will help you to know about your language skills.

Directions : As children, we must know how to communicate with elders, strangers, friends, etc., in a sweet manner. Given below are some situations. Choose the option which you feel is correct in every case.

1. Your uncle and aunt have come for dinner. You help your mother to serve. Your aunt thanks you. You reply :
   (i) It's okay.
   (ii) Thank you !
   (iii) It's my pleasure !

2. Your elder brother has joined Merchant Navy. He is going on his first trip abroad. You wish him :
   (i) All the best !
   (ii) Bon voyage !
   (iii) Good luck !

3. An old friend meets you after several years. You say :
   (i) What a pleasant surprise !
   (ii) Hello !
   (iii) How are you !

4. You are unable to hear your teacher's instruction as you are sitting at the back of the class. You stand up and say:
   (i) I'm sorry.
   (ii) I beg your pardon.
   (iii) What ?

5. You have to give a speech in the class. The class is noisy. You say:
   (i) Shut up !
   (ii) Quiet every one!
   (iii) May I have your attention please!

6. It is New Year's Day. Your friend wishes you, "A Happy New Year." You say:
   (i) Happy New Year !
   (ii) Same to you !
   (iii) Welcome !

7. Your grandfather has come to visit you for a few days. As he is leaving, you may touch his feet and say :
   (i) Goodbye grandfather !
   (ii) May you live long grandfather !
   (iii) Give me your blessings grandfather !

8. Your grandmother is not well. You visit her in the hospital. What will you say?
   (i) Get well soon, granny !
   (ii) May God bless you, granny !
   (iii) All is well, granny !

9. If you are talking to someone and in between the conversation you sneeze, you say :
   (i) Do not bother !
   (ii) Excuse me !
   (iii) Carry on with your conversation.

10. You dash into somebody, you say :
   (i) Sorry !
   (ii) You must watch out when you walk!
   (iii) What are you upto?

Spoken and Written Expression

LEARNING OBJECTIVES

This lesson will help you to

- learn to write proper answers.
- understand the sentence and answer accordingly.

INTRODUCTION

It goes without saying that a language is made up of words arranged in a proper manner to make sentences. If the sentences are not framed properly, the listener or the reader will not be able to understand what we are trying to convey. Language is a medium to communicate with people. English has now become a world language. If we are able to read, write and speak in English then rest assured, we can go anywhere in this world and we will be able to convey what we want to say.

Like in any other language, in English also we need to follow certain rules. If we use wrong words then it will convey a wrong expression. Like if I say that I have going to the museum. Does it sound meaningful? No, it does not! clarify whether you are going or have been to the museum.

To gain mastery over any language one need to consistently practise the language. Listen to people who speak English.

Try to watch your favourite T.V programmes in English.

Try to read as much literature in English as you can. While reading if you come across words, of which you

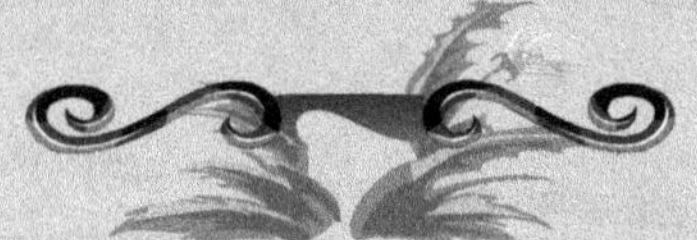

❖ Practice makes a man perfect

The more you speak, the more proficient you will become in this language. Even if you go wrong somewhere, don't get disheartened, Keep trying.

don't know meaning, look for them in the dictionary.

Some dictionaries tell you how to pronounce a word.

Always remember no one can be perfect, so you have to keep trying.

Learn the basic rules of grammar.

When your tap is not working

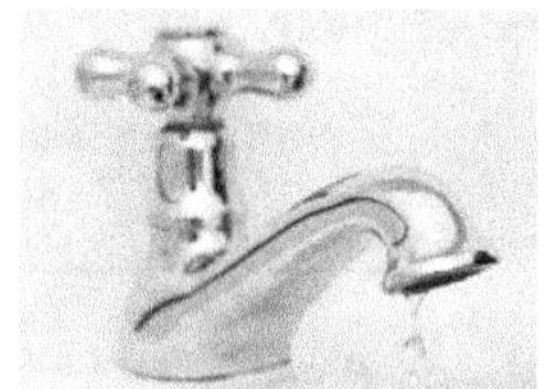

Mrs. Paula: The tap is leaking.
Mr. Paul: I think we must call a plumber immediately.

When you meet someone on road

Mohan: Hello, Shyam. It has been a long time since we met. How are you?
Shyam: I am fine, how are you?

A visit to a doctor

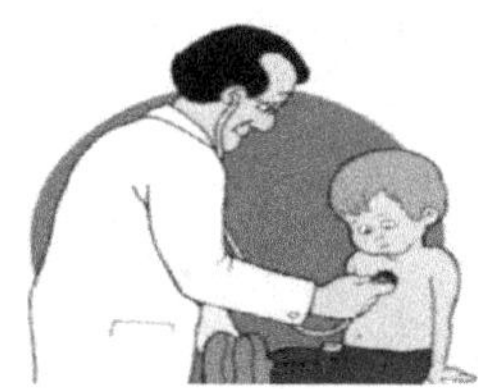

Patient: Good morning, doctor !
Doctor: Good morning, what's wrong with you?
Patient: I've been suffering from fever since yesterday.

At a Hotel Reception

Receptionist: Sir, May I help you.
Customer : Yes, I want a room.

A telephonic conversation

Hello, who's calling?
Hello I am Ryan. May I speak to Paul?

Multiple Choice Questions

LEVEL – 1

Directions (Qs. 1–15): Read the following sentences and fill in the blanks from the options given below

1. Jane: I was planning a trip to Goa during the summer vacation   **(2012)**

   Davis: ________________________________

   (a)   What are you saying? What happened?

   (b)   What a coincidence! Even I was discussing the same trip yesterday.

   (c)   This house is mine.

   (d)   No, I had gone there yesterday.

2. **Do you have any hobby?**   **(2013)**

   (a)   Yes, I like playing chess and reading.

   (b)   My mom is not well.

   (c)   The postman has delivered this parcel

   (d)   My school is too far.

3. **What do you do?**

   (a)   This pen belongs to me.   (b)   I am into property business.

   (c)   My Dad bought this car for me.   (d)   I don't like going for an outing.

4. **Good morning, Sir. May I help you?**

   (a)   I am going for a picnic.

   (b)   No, My Mom has told me not to go there.

   (c)   Yes, do you have split A.C's?

   (d)   He's too clumsy!

5. **What did your Mom say? Can we go?**   **(2014)**

   (a)   Mom said that I am a great cyclist.

   (b)   Mom said that we can go, but will have to come early

   (c)   His mother is very strict, she will not allow.

   (d) My mom is not well.

6. **Hello, Karen. How are you feeling today?**   (2012)

   Karen: _________________________ .

   (a) He is sleeping.

   (b) Much better, thanks for asking.

   (c) She is playing in the park

   (d) I don't know, I will go.

7. **Hello, Harry. It's my birthday today. I am throwing a party at my place. Will you come?**

   Harry: _________________________ .   (2015)

   (a) Thanks for inviting me. Many many happy returns of the day. Yes I will come

   (b) What did you say, its very tough to understand.

   (c) His Dad is very busy today.

   (d) I will buy flowers for decoration.

8. **Do you know, What is the date today?**

   (a) Of course. Today is 30th March   (b) What did he say?

   (c) My mom is a very good cook   (d) Yes, its very tough to tell.

9. **Tom: Ms. Jane, is it your first trip to Mumbai?**

   Jane: _________________________ .   (2016)

   (a) That picture is so beautiful.

   (b) I'll like to have a cup of tea.

   (c) Yes, everything is new to me. Mumbai is lovely.

   (d) The doctor is just coming.

10. **The scenery out there is so beautiful.**

(a) How much do we have to walk?   (b) Yes, the scenery is beautiful.

(c) Will you give me your car?   (d) I don't like to go there.

11. **Rosa: Will you take my photograph, Miss Nina?**   (2016)

Nina: ___________________________

(a) No, I left it somewhere   (b) The flowers are so beautiful!

(c) Of course. It is my pleasure.   (d) Thank you so much.

12. **Hari: Will you come to Ooty for a trip next year?**   (2014)

Tom: ___________________________________.

(a) What are you saying?

(b) Do not mention, please.

(c) Goodbye and thanks for taking care of me.

(d) Oh, yes. I should be there early in May next year.

13. **Did you read today's newspaper?**

(a) Yes, I have read it.   (b) I wanted to, but could not go.

(c) His father is a news reporter.   (d) Wow! You drove so well.

14. **Shopkeeper: Your bill is of Rs.150.**   (2012)

Customer:___________________________

(a) Ok, but my house is very far.

(b) Ok, I'll just pay.

(c) I don't believe it!

(d) It's not that easy, as it seems to you.

15. **Hello, is it 66004499?**   (2013)

(a) No, I am Neha.

(b) Yes, my house is very close.

(c) Yes, it is. May I know who's calling?

(d) Thanks for calling.

Directions (Qs. 16-20) : Look at the picture and choose the correct option to complete the conversation.

16.   **(2014)**

(a) No, I am sleepy.   (b) Yes.

(c) Yes, Mummy.   (d) No, I don't like to.

17.   **(2015)**

(a) You are a good boy   (b) I don't believe you

(c) You should not do that.   (d) It's raining

18.

(a) Hello! Sam.   (b) Goodbye, Sam.

(c) Good morning, Sam.   (d) Thank you, Sam.

19.

(a) Goodbye, Swati.

(b) Welcome, Swati.

(c) Happy Birthday, Swati.

(d) None of these.

20.

(2016)

(a) Good night, Tom.

(b) Goodbye, Tom.

(c) Thank you, Tom.

(d) Hello, who is speaking?

Choose the most suitable option to complete each conversation.

21. Dev : Wow! This is boring.   (2018)

    Brad : I know. I _________ seem to stay awake.

    (a) can't   (b) don't   (c) shan't   (d) won't

22. Troy : Here is my _______ bookbag that I got at the weekend.   (2018)

    Ralph : Wow, it's big!

    (a) already   (b) brothers   (c) new   (d) car

23. Ed : I've got to up earlier _________ I am always late.   (2018)

    (a) just   (b) until   (c) so   (d) because

24. Shonna : Can you pass me my pen, please ?

    Sam : Yeah, _______________.   (2018)

    (a) never him   (b) sure thing

    (c) always happy   (d) perhaps over here

25. Arthur : Our new maths book is the __________ I've ever seen!   (2018)

    (a) easiest   (b) wettest

    (c) richest   (d) saddest

Directions (Q. No. 26 to 30): Choose the most suitable option to complete each conversation.

> **Example**
>
> Jay : Can I come and play with you tomorrow
> Anita : Yeah, _____________.
> (a) Please do   (b) I want
> (c) let's go   (d) up standing

26. Raheem : I got __________ job offer from LHC.   (2020)

    Aman : That's great! Congratulations.
    (a) the   (b) a
    (c) no   (d) any

27. Joe : I've been working so hard, I need a __________.   (2020)
    (a) dance   (b) vacation
    (c) work   (d) relax

28. Raj : This is the worst time.
    Reena : Don't worry. Every cloud has a __________ lining.   (2020)
    (a) thin   (b) silver
    (c) golden   (d) bronze

29. Francis : How was the movie?   (2020)
    Geetu : It was __________. I really enjoyed it.
    (a) Ok   (b) boring
    (c) rough   (d) fantastic

30. Person 1 : Do you have __________ idea about the bus-stop?   (2020)
    Person 2 : No, I am new here.
    (a) much   (b) many
    (c) any   (d) most

LEVEL – 2

Directions (Qs. 1–11): Read the conversation given below and fill in the blanks from the options given below.   **[Critical Thinking]**

Today was 25th December, Jenny was really excited. It was Christmas Day today. Her father had decorated the Christmas Tree. One of her friends, Soniya had come over, She asked", "When did you do these decorations"

Jenny answered(1)"_______________________". Soniya became more curious, she again asked" Then who did them?". Jenny replied(2)_______________________.He does them every year."

Soniya again asked(3)" _______________________"?

To which Jenny replied "I do the gift wrapping. I did it last year also."

Soniya asked Jenny" What does your mother do on Christmas"?

Jenny replied(4) " _______________________."

Soniya asked "Does she make good Christmas cakes"?

Jenny replied(5)"_______________________".

Soniya said "I love Christmas cakes".

Jenny said(6)"_______________________."

Soniya asked Jenny "What all do you do during Christmas"? Do you go to the church"?

Jenny replied (7)"_______________________"

Soniya Said "Oh! That's really good. She again asked'(8)_______________________?"

"We exchange gifts when we visit each other". Jenny replied.

"Do you also sing Christmas carols?" Soniya wanted to know.

(9)_"_______________________"Jenny said.

"That means celebrating Christmas is great fun!" Soniya was really excited now.

(10)_______________________Jenny was equally excited.

"Merry Christmas Jenny" Soniya wished Jenny.

Jenny also said"(11)_______________________.

1. (a) "I did not do them"

    (b) "That is not my job, I will not do it"

    (c) "My mom is not well"

    (d) "See I bought a new car for myself"

2. (a) "His mom called me today"

    (b) " I am going for dinner tonight"

    (c) " My father did them"

    (d) "These are my gifts"

3. (a) "My Mom is a great cook"

    (b) "This is a globe, do you know that"

    (c) "What do you do to help him"

    (d) "That garden is so lovely"

4. (a) "We all go to the Church'

    (b) "She does cooking"

    (c) "He is a great singer. Let's listen to his songs"

    (d) "Why should I give my shoes to you"

5. (a) "Does she make good clothes"

    (b) "Go to the cobbler and get shoes mended"

    (c) "There is an earthquake in that city"

    (d) "Yes, she does"

6. (a) "Do you know what it takes to buy a new car"

    (b) "She has done her job quite well"

    (c) "I love them too"

    (d) "I can make good cards"

7. (a) "Yes, we all go to the church'

    (b) "Why would I"

    (c) "No, it's my mom's job"

    (d) "Why don't you also go, it's going to be great fun"

8. (a) "What is it all about"

    (b) "We exchange gifts "

    (c) "When do you exchange gifts"

    (d) "Why should I tell you"

9.   (a) "That's really tough to do"

    (b) "Yes , we sing Christmas carols."

    (c) My brother does it better."

    (d) "Dad will come and tell you"

10. (a) "yes, it's very slow"

    (b) "Yes, only if you want to go"

    (c) "Yes, it is".

    (d) "No, he has not taken my car."

11. (a) "Happy Birthday to you"

    (b) "Merry Christmas to you too!"

    (c) "What are you doing? It will spoil the whole thing."

    (d) "You've done a great job"

Directions (Qs. 12–22): Read the following conversation based on a story and fill in the blanks from the options given below.   **(2015)**

The Lion And The Rabbit

Narrator: Once upon a time in a jungle. The lion has fixed up a day for each animal to be eaten by it. This time is the turn of a rabbit.

Lion: (roars)" I will eat you right away."

Rabbit: No, you can't.

Lion (laughs) (12)"_________________. "Are you (13) _____________?"

Rabbit: No, (14)______ all.

Lion: Are you joking? Or you have gone mad because of your fear of dying.

Rabbit:" I am (15)_______________."

Narrator: By now the lion is also wondering as to what has gone wrong to the rabbit.

Lion: "(16) _________ die."

Rabbit: Wait... I am Calling my friend.

Lion:' Friend?(17)________________friend".

Rabbit: Okay, I will take you there.

Narrator: The lion starts following the rabbit.

Lion : where does he stay?

Rabbit: "He (18)______________a well."

Narrator: They reach near a well.

Rabbit: He looks into well.

Narrator: The rabbit looks inside the well.

Rabbit: See_(19)"________________there".

Narrator: The lion looks inside, it sees it's own reflection and thinks that there is another lion that stays in that well.

Lion roars (20)."__________________"_

It's voice echoes"(21)________________"

Narrator: The same voice comes back. This really makes the lion angry and it jumps into the well.

Narrator: This story teaches us that_(22)__________________.

12.	(a)	"Give you my car"	(b)	"what are you saying"
	(c)	"can I help you"	(d)	"Oh! Good you are here"
13.	(a)	"not scared"	(b)	"No I can't do anything"
	(c)	"Where is that hunter"?	(d)	"Call your mom"
14.	(a)	"Nobody can help you"	(b)	"It is so scary"
	(c)	Not at	(d)	"It's his problem."
15.	(a)	"This is not my house"	(b)	"This is a jungle"
	(c)	not scared of dying	(d)	"It's his work, let him do it"
16.	(a)	"It's not easy"	(b)	"I found it quite easy".
	(c)	"Get ready to	(d)	"No, you can't eat me .
17.	(a)	"who's your	(b)	I can't do that. It is tough
	(c)	"What are you saying?"	(d)	No, that's so difficult to do.
18.	(a)	"cut the cake".	(b)	"stays in a"
	(c)	"ate the cake"	(d)	"Are You okay"?
19.	(a)	"Why did you do this?"	(b)	"it stays"
	(c)	"No, It wasn't your job….	(d)	"my pleasure…
20.	(a)	Who is there?	(b)	Left me to….
	(c)	"Protected that dog's…	(d)	"No one save your….

21. (a) "Thanks, I am okay now… (b) "Who is there?

    (c) "Please don't say that .. (d) "I love to do my…

22. (a) always use your wisdom. (b) Never get caught up in a net.

    (c) Never challenge a lion. (d) Never go to a well.

Directions (Qs. 23–30): Read the following passage about safety precautions and fill in the blanks from the options given below. (*Critical Thinking, 2014*)

Today our class teacher did not teach us, but she told us a few safety precautions.

She told us to stay away from fire because (23) ___________________

us. She told us, not to touch an electric switch (24) ________because

(25) ______________. In a moving vehicle, she told us not to (26)

____________window because (27)____________. I should look

at (28) __________road before, (29)___________________ that

(30)________way.

23. (a) it can burn
    (b) Help me
    (c) give me heat
    (d) Cook food for me

24. (a) go and eat good food
    (b) it's great to be here
    (c) with Wet hands
    (d) she will go and teach another class.

25. (a) electricity is very good
    (b) she was leaving from work

    (c)   we can get an electric shock
    (d)   he would hire a driver to drive his car

26. (a)   he is a great chef, why don't you hire him?
    (b)   my Mom will not like my going out like this.
    (c)   try to practise driving.
    (d)   take our hand or head out of the

27. (a)   his mom baked a cake on her anniversary.
    (b)   this is his pet dog.
    (c)   you can get hurt.
    (d)   you mean cricket

28. (a)   do not look out of the window.
    (b)   we can't go now , it is raining
    (c)   both the sides of the
    (d)   oops! I missed it again.

29. (a)   crossing the road to make sure
    (b)   sorry, I have to rush, I am already late.
    (c)   the tap is leaking, call up the plumber.
    (d)   hurray! I came first in the race.

30. (a)   that car is mine
    (b)   no vehicle is coming our
    (c)   he has rented his house to a family
    (d)   i have seen a lion roaring

For questions 31 to 35, choose the most suitable option to complete each conversation.
(2019)

Example :

Jay : Can I come and play with you tomorrow ?

Anita : Yeah, _________________.

(a) please do   (b) I want   (c) let's go   (d) up standing

31. Ismael : Are you having lunch in the canteen today ?

    Ellis : I'm _________. But probably, that's where I normally eat.

    (a) very keen   (b) absolute   (c) not sure   (d) for real

32. Akbar : My parents don't have a TV in the house anymore!

    Sophia : Really, I wish I didn't _________ my time just staring at ours.

    (a) plan   (b) give   (c) waste   (d) remove

33. Yan : We need to get going soon, Inga.

    Inga : Yes, of course, I _________ forgot about the time.

    (a) enormously   (b) emptily   (c) completely   (d) breakingly

34. Gulshan : What's going on here?

    Diniz : _________, but there are a lot of people standing around watching.

    (a) No way   (b) Not much

    (c) Never again   (d) Not a chance

35. Elham : Traditionally, my family always has a large meal that night.

    Fahad : Oh, really, my family just relaxes and _________ take away.

    (a) move   (b) do   (c) plays   (d) gets

36. Choose the most suitable option to complete the conversation.   (2020)
    Mother : Finish what's on your plate.
    Soma : Mom, the curry is very spicy, I can _________ eat it.
    (a) always   (b) barely
    (c) almost   (d) easy

Directions (Qs. 37-41): Look at the picture and choose the correct answer.

37. It is an image of a _________ .   (2021)
    (a) class   (b) party
    (c) safari   (d) zoo cage

38. All the people in the jeep have ________   (2021)
    (a) cameras   (b) sunglasses
    (c) hats   (d) bags

39. ________ is driving the jeep.   (2021)
    (a) Sonu   (b) Ginni
    (c) Rahul   (d) None

40. They look ______ to see a tiger.   (2021)
    (a) scared   (b) excited
    (c) terrified   (d) sad

41. There is/are ______ around them.   (2021)
    (a) animals   (b) people
    (c) greenery   (d) stars

42. Choose the correct option to complete the conversation.   (2021)
    Zara : I feel like eating a pizza ________.
    Zafar : Let's go and get it.
    (a) sudden   (b) suddenly
    (c) then   (d) how

Directions (Qs. 43-47): Look at the picture and choose the correct answer.

43. Mom and Dad are looking ______ each other.   (2022)
    (a) up   (b) at
    (c) of   (d) in

44. Anjali is holding a ________ in her hands.   (2022)
    (a) football   (b) teddy bear
    (c) balloon   (d) box

45. There is a _______ sitting on the bench.   (2022)

   (a) woman   (b) child

   (c) man   (d) bird

46. Which fruit is not there in the picture?   (2022)

   (a) Pineapple   (b) Banana

   (c) Watermelon   (d) Apple

47. Which of the following is in a pair?   (2022)

   (a) Mat   (b) Racket

   (c) Banana   (d) Football

Directions (Qs. 48-52): Choose the correct option to complete each conversation.

48. Preeti: 1 like Ananya's sense _______ humour.   (2022)
Pinki: Me too.

   (a) on   (b) of

   (c) at   (d) up

49. Nancy: During Christmas, the malls are very _______ .   (2022)

   (a) crowdful   (b) crowd

   (c) crowded   (d) crowds

50. Jatin: You _______ watched this movie, have you?   (2022)
Ram: Yes, I have.

   (a) hadn't   (b) wasn't

   (c) aren't   (d) haven't

51. Radha: I am sorry. I am _______ my words back.
Gagan: It's alright.   (2022)

   (a) take   (b) took

   (c) taken   (d) taking

52. Tania: Nina always makes _______ false stories about everyone in the class.
                          (2022)

   (a) up   (b) down

   (c) to   (d) in

53. Choose the correct option to complete the conversation.   (2022)
Dad: Are you learning _______ French at school?
Son: Yes, I am.

   (a) a   (b) an

   (c) the   (d) no article

RESPONSE GRID

LEVEL 1

1. a b c d 2. a b c d 3. a b c d 4. a b c d 5. a b c d
6. a b c d 7. a b c d 8. a b c d 9. a b c d 10. a b c d
11. a b c d 12. a b c d 13. a b c d 14. a b c d 15. a b c d
16. a b c d 17. a b c d 18. a b c d 19. a b c d 20. a b c d
21. a b c d 22. a b c d 23. a b c d 24. a b c d 25. a b c d
26. a b c d 27. a b c d 28. a b c d 29. a b c d 30. a b c d

LEVEL 2

1. a b c d 2. a b c d 3. a b c d 4. a b c d 5. a b c d
6. a b c d 7. a b c d 8. a b c d 9. a b c d 10. a b c d
11. a b c d 12. a b c d 13. a b c d 14. a b c d 15. a b c d
16. a b c d 17. a b c d 18. a b c d 19. a b c d 20. a b c d
21. a b c d 22. a b c d 23. a b c d 24. a b c d 25. a b c d
26. a b c d 27. a b c d 28. a b c d 29. a b c d 30. a b c d
31. a b c d 32. a b c d 33. a b c d 34. a b c d 35. a b c d
36. a b c d 37. a b c d 38. a b c d 39. a b c d 40. a b c d
41. a b c d 42. a b c d 43. a b c d 44. a b c d 45. a b c d
46. a b c d 47. a b c d 48. a b c d 49. a b c d 50. a b c d
51. a b c d 52. a b c d 53. a b c d

Solutions with Explanation

LEVEL - 1

1. **(b)** Jane: I was planning a trip to Goa during the summer vacation

   Davis: What a coincidence! Even I was discussing the same trip yesterday.

2. **(a)**   Do you have any hobby?

    Yes, I like playing chess and reading.

3. **(b)**   What do you do?

    I am into property business.   .

4. **(c)**   Sales Girl: Good morning, Sir. May I help you?.

    Customer: Yes, do you have split A.C's?

5. **(b)**   What did your Mom say? Can we go?

    Mom said that we can go, but will have to come early.

6. **(b)**   Hello, Karen. How are you feeling today?

    Much better, thanks for asking.

7. **(a)**   Hello, Harry. It's my birthday today. I am throwing a party at my place. Will you come?

    Thanks for inviting me. Many-many happy returns of the day. Yes I will come

8. **(a)**   Do you know, What is the date today?

    Of course. Today is 30th March

9. **(c)**   Tom: Ms. Jane, is it your first trip to Mumbai?

    Jane: Yes, everything is new to me. Mumbai is lovely.

10. **(b)**   The scenery out there is so beautiful.

    Yes, the scenery is beautiful.

11. **(c)**   Rosa: Will you take my photograph, Miss Nina?

    Nina: Of course. It is my pleasure

12. **(d)**   Hari: Will you come to Ooty for a trip next year?

    Tom: Oh, yes. I should be there early in May next year.

13. **(a)**   Did you read today's newspaper?

    Yes, I have read it.

14. **(b)**   Shopkeeper: Your bill is of Rs.150 .

    Customer: Ok, I'll just pay.

15. **(c)**   Hello, is it 66004499?

    Yes, it is. May I know who's calling?

16. **(c)**   Yes, mummy

17. **(a)**   You are a good boy

18. **(b)**   Goodbye, Sam

19. (c) Happy Birthday, Swati
20. (c) Thank you, Tom
21. (a) can't
22. (c) new
23. (d) because
24. (b) sure thing
25. (a) easiest
26. (a) a
27. (c) vacation
28. (b) silver
29. (d) fantastic
30. (c) any

LEVEL – 2

1.   (a) "I did not do them"
2.   (c) "My father did them"
3.   (c) "What do you do to help him"
4.   (b) "She does cooking'
5.   (d) "Yes, she does"
6.   (c) " I love them too!
7.   (a) "Yes, we all go to the church'
8.   (c) "When do you exchange gifts"
9.   (b) "Yes , we sing Christmas carols."
10. (c) "Yes, it is".
11. (b) "Merry Christmas to you too"
12   (b) "what are you saying"
13. (a) "not scared"
14. (c) No, not at
15. (c) not scared of dying
16. (c) "get ready to
17. (a) " who's your
18. (b) stays in a"
19. (b) "it stays
20. (a) Who is there?
21. (b) "who is there?
22. (a) always use your wisdom.

23.	**(a)**	it can burn
24.	**(c)**	with wet hands
25.	**(c)**	we can get an electric shock
26.	**(d)**	take our hand or head out of the
27.	**(c)**	you can get hurt
28.	**(c)**	both the sides of the.
29.	**(a)**	crossing the road to make sure
30.	**(b)**	no vehicle is coming our
31.	**(c)**	not sure
32.	**(c)**	waste
33.	**(c)**	completely
34.	**(b)**	Not much
35.	**(d)**	gets
36.	**(b)**	barely
37.	**(c)**	It is an image of a safari.
38.	**(c)**	The people in the image are shown to have hats.
39.	**(c)**	Rahul is driving the jeep.
40.	**(b)**	They look excited to see a tiger.
41.	**(c)**	There is greenery around them.
42.	**(b)**	I feel like eating a pizza suddenly.
43.	**(b)**	Mom and dad are looking at each other.
44.	**(a)**	Anjali is holding a football in her hand.
45.	**(c)**	There is a man sitting on the bench.
46.	**(a)**	Pineapple is not there in the picture.
47.	**(b)**	Rackets are shown in pair in the picture.
48.	**(b)**	I like Ananya's sense of humour.
49.	**(c)**	The malls are very crowded.
50.	**(d)**	You haven't watched this movie, have you?
51.	**(d)**	I am taking my words back.
52.	**(a)**	Nina always makes up false stories about everyone in the class.
53.	**(a)**	No article is used after the verb ending with –ing.

<table><tr><td>15</td><td></td></tr></table>

15 CHAPTER FOREWORD

The subject of discussion of this chapter is comprehension.

Comprehension means understanding what you are reading. It can be related to any type of written material such as passage, poem, report, articles etc.

Here is an exercise which is based on reading comprehension.

Directions : Read the following poem and answer the questions that follow.

THE ROSE

It is a red rose,
It stands for love
I want to pluck it
I shall give it to my
teacher
She will love it

The rose is smiling
So red, so beautiful
It smells good
I have plucked it
I will give to my teacher
She will be very happy

1. What colour is the rose?
   ____

2. What does 'it' stand for?
   ____

3 Who does the poet want to give the rose to?
   ____
   ____

4. Why do you think he wants to do so?
   ____
   ____
   ____

5. What is the rose doing?
   ____
   ____
   ____

15 Chapter

Comprehension

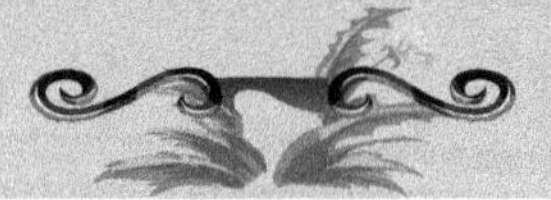

LEARNING OBJECTIVES

This lesson will help you to-

- understand what is comprehension all about.
- find information from the passage
- answer the questions asked thereafter
- build confidence

INTRODUCTION

Let's do comprehension today. Do you all know anything about comprehension?

Comprehension is understanding, and then answering the questions based on the passage that you have read

- Comprehension is your ability to understand what is written. It also means to gain meaning from what is read.
- Reading comprehension is one of the pillars of the act of reading.
- The passages can have any topic as the theme. A single topic can be presented in different ways.
- Reading comprehension is making a meaning of word and trying to understand the written text.
- A comprehension can be a passage or a poem, that needs to be understood to the level of being able to answer the questions that are based only on that passage or that poem.
- Writers don't always tell you what they think or believe or why they have written the text. Sometimes you have to try to think like they do and work it out for yourself.
- When we read, we often decide what we think might be true based on information in the text. This is called inferring.

STEPS

- First read the passage carefully.
- Try to understand the passage.
- Read each question carefully, so that you understand exactly what you are being asked to do before you begin.

FOUNDATIONS

- Conceptual Knowledge: Children must be familiar with the various concepts and be clear in them.
- Language skills: Children must be familiar with the language so that they do not get stuck at any word.
- Text features: you must know that the title, and the pictures provided are all related to the text

Comprehension can be tough when you are not so familiar with the words and it will take too much of your time to try to pronounce the word correctly. Sight reading or ability to recognize words makes comprehension easier

STRATEGIES

1. Make sure you understand what you read.
2. learn how to work out the main idea and why it is important. There are often many ideas in a text but there is one idea that joins the other ideas together. This is the main idea.
3. Read the text then ask yourself, "what is it mainly about"?
4. The title is a very good clue to the main idea because a good title often tells the reader what the text is about.
5. The answers are usually not in the text, but there is information to give you clues to think about it.

Multiple Choice Questions

LEVEL – 1

Directions (Qs. 1–5): Read the passages carefully and then answer from the options given below. (2012)

Harry was very happy today. His parents were taking him out to a picnic. They were going out to the Deer Park .Harry was very excited. He called up all his friends to tell them about it. All his friends were also very excited about it, they also wanted to come along. Harry wanted to take five of his friends with him. He went to ask his Dad about it, who agreed. They had a big car. In the morning all of them got together at Harry's place and left for picnic. They took cricket bat, football and other outdoor games with them.

1. **Why was Harry happy?**

   (a)   Because it was his birthday.

   (b)   Because his father bought him new bat.

   (c)   Because his father was taking him out for picnic.

   (d)   Because he came first in class.

2. **Where was Harry going for picnic?**

   (a)   India Gate

   (b)   Nearby park

   (c)   Deer park

   (d)   Botanical Garden

3. **How many friends did Harry want to take with him?**

   (a)   Two

   (b)   Five

   (c)   Eight

   (d)   One

4. **What did they take with them?**

   (a)   Outdoor games

   (b)   Chess, Ludo

   (c)   Chips and burgers

   (d)   Vegetables

5. **The antonym of big is __________.**

   (a)   small

   (b)   large

   (c)   tall

   (d)   short

Directions (Qs. 6–10): Read the passage given below and answer the questions from the options given below. (2014)

Eid

The festival of Eid was approaching. Aslam's father gave him Eidi (money on account of Eid) so that he could enjoy with his friends. His father gave him thousand rupees. His mother too gave him some money. Aslam had a total of ₹2000 cash.

Aslam wanted to celebrate Eid in a different manner. He thought that he and his friends would have a lot of fun at home. He would treat his friends to the sweets that his mother had made, but was figuring out as to what he would do with the money. He thought of spending the money in doing some good, noble work.

6. **What is Eidi?**

   (a) Sweets of Eid
   (b) Gifts of birthday
   (c) Money given on Eid
   (d) None of the above

7. **Why did Aslam's father give him Eidi?**

   (a) To see a movie
   (b) To go for the picnic
   (c) To enjoy with friends
   (d) To give it back to his mother

8. **Aslam wanted to celebrate Eid in __________.**

   (a) a different way
   (b) a grand way
   (c) a funny manner
   (d) none of the above

9. **Aslam thought to treat his friends to __________.**

   (a) lots of sweets from market
   (b) the sweets made by his mother
   (c) the sweets made by neighbours
   (d) none of the above

10. **Aslam wanted to spend his Eidi __________.**

   (a) on his clothes
   (b) on toys
   (c) on gifts for friends
   (d) in doing some noble work

Directions (Qs. 11–15) : Read the passage carefully and answer the questions based on adjectives.

Manav has a _____(11) pet dog. Its ears are very _____(12). Its fur is _____(13) and soft. Everyday he gives the dog _____(14) bones to chew. It runs very _____(15).

11. (a) big   (b) huge   (c) small   (d) ugly

12. (a) big   (b) long   (c) short   (d) heavy

13. (a) red   (b) white   (c) dark   (d) heavy

14. (a) bold   (b) fresh   (c) many   (d) four

15. (a) slow   (b) fastly   (c) fast   (d) quick

Directions (Qs. 16–20): Read the passage given below and answer the questions from the options given below. (2016)

The Unhappy King

Many years ago, there lived a king. He possessed a beautiful and enormous palace. He ate delicious food , wore silky clothes but still he was unhappy. He decided to ask his ministers how he could become happy.

He always thought of doing something or the other to make himself happy. He invited wise men from all over to his kingdom to suggest ways to make him happy. All of them came and suggested one or the other way to make him happy. One of them said you wear the shoes of a happy man and you will be happy. Another man said that you make friends with people and be happy. All these answers did not satisfy the king. So he decided to take round of his kingdom. While he was wandering in his chariot , he saw a group of boys, working in a farm. They were all very happy. He went up to them and asked" why are you so happy?". One of the boys said "we are happy to work together". Now the king came to know the secret of happiness.

16. What did the king eat?

   (a) Pizza and burger   (b) Salad

   (c) Fruits and vegetables   (d) Delicious food

17. Whom did the king invite to his court?

   (a) The princess.   (b) The animals.

   (c) The ministers.   (d) The wise men of his kingdom.

18. Whom did he see while wandering?

   (a) A wise man.   (b) An old man.

   (c) A group of boys.   (d) A prince.

19. What were the boys doing?

   (a) Playing in the park.   (b) Working in their farm.

   (c) Fighting with each other.   (d) Running together.

20. Why were the boys so happy?

    (a)   Because they were playing together.

    (b)   Because they were working together.

    (c)   Because they were eating good food.

    (d)   Because they had become kings.

Directions (Q. No. 21 to 25): Read the passage and answer the questions that follow.

Tibet is a part of western China. The capital of Tibet is Lhasa.

Most of Tibet is on a piece of land called the Qinghai-Tibet Plateau. The plateau is a raised flat area about 15,000 feet (4,600 meters) above sea level. Tibet is so high that it is often called the Roof of the World. The Himalayan Mountains are to the south. Tibet's climate is cold and dry. The climate is generally dry since it is protected by mountain barriers from monsoons.

Tibetans speak the Tibetan language and practice their own form of Buddhism. The Dalai and the Panchen Lamas are the main leaders of Tibetan Buddhism. Main religion of Tibet is Buddhism. Their traditions make it a place of interest to many people. The local monks are sometimes said to have special, super human abilities.

Due to limited arable land, livestock raising is the primary occupation on the Tibetan Plateau. Among those raised are sheep, cattle, goats, camels, yaks, donkeys, and horses. They grow barley, wheat, millet, buckwheat, and potatoes. Tibetans also make handicrafts such as carpets, blankets, jewelry, and wooden bowls. A few factories produce textiles,

21. The capital of Tibet is called ___________.   (2020)

    (a) China

    (b) Himalaya

    (c) Lhasa

    (d) Panchen

> **Example**
>
> The passage is about ________.
>
> (a) (Tibet)   (b) India
>
> (c) Sheep   (d) Chine

22. The Himalayan Mountain are to the _________ of Tibet.   (2020)

    (a) north   (b) south

    (c) east   (d) west

23. The climate of Tibet is dry because _________.   (2020)

    (a) it is surrounded by deserts

    (b) it is at high altitude

    (c) it is protected by mountain barriers from monsoon

    (d) the land is cold

24. Livestock is the primary occupation on the Tibetan Plateau because _________.

(2020)

    (a) of plenty of grazing land   (b) of large number of cattle stock

    (c) there is limited arable land   (d) of their religion

25. Tibetans mainly grow barley, wheat, millet, buckwheat and __________.

(2020)

    (a) cotton   (b) mustard

    (c) potatoest   (d) rice

LEVEL – 2

Directions (Qs. 1–5): Read the passages given below and answer the questions from the options given below (Tricky)

The Rich Man And The Poor Man

Once upon a time there was a very rich man. He was the richest man in the whole of India. He was a very shrewd person. He did the business of lending money to people, and would fool everyone. One day a man came to him for loan, he wholeheartedly agreed to provide him with loan. But told him, that he will have to pay double the amount after one month. The poor man was in a dire need of money, so he agreed. After about one month, the rich moneylender went to the poor man's house to ask for his money back or pay double amount. The poor man did not have a single penny with him. But the moneylender would not leave him now. He told that poor man to pay the money through his services. That day onwards the poor man started working in the moneylender's house.

1. The rich man was a very _______.

    (a) nice person   (b) shrewd person

    (c) kind person   (d) honest person

2. What did the rich man do?

    (a) Sell sweets   (b) Lend money

    (c) Stitch clothes   (d) Mend shoes

3. **How much interest was the poor man required to pay?**
   (a) No money   (b) Double   (c) Triple   (d) One rupee

4. **What is the opposite of lend?**
   (a) Buy   (b) Sell   (c) Borrow   (d) Share

5. **How did the poor man pay back his money?**
   (a) He gave him back his money   (b) He had to work for the rich man.
   (c) He sold his land   (d) He sold his house

Directions (Qs. 6–11): Read the poem given below and answer the questions from the options given below (2015)

Mouse and Cat

The mouse said to the cat,
away,
will not come out from the hole,
Stay away.
There is so much to eat,
Look around,
I am scared of you
Go away
I am hungry too!
But cannot come out of the hole
Stay away
The cat said to the mouse
You are my favorite meal,
I can't stay away
You better come out,
I will not go away.

6. **Why does the mouse want cat to go away?**
   (a) Because it is scared of it.   (b) Because it wants to play.
   (c) Because it is sad.   (d) Because it has to go somewhere.

7. **Where has the mouse hidden itself?**
   (a) Behind the curtain.   (b) Under the table.
   (c) In a hole.   (d) In a cupboard.

8. **According to you where is the cat?**
   (a) In the park.   (b) In the room.
   (c) In the kitchen.   (d) Outside the hole.

9. **What is rhyming word for meal?**

    (a) Peal   (b) Teal   (c) Keel   (d) Seel

10. **What will the cat do, once the mouse comes out?**

    (a) It will start playing with it.   (b) It will eat the mouse.

    (c) It will study with the mouse   (d) it will go out with the mouse.

11. **Why do you think cat and mouse cannot be friends?**

    (a) Because the cat will eat the mouse

    (b) Because the mouse will be scared of the cat.

    (c) Because cat's favorite food is a mouse

    (d) All of the above

Directions (Qs. 12-17): Read the passage given below and answer the questions from the options given below.   **(Critical Thinking, 2016)**

KAREN's DOLL

Karen was very sad today. Her father had refused to buy her a new doll. All her friends had bought new dolls for themselves, but Karen's father did not buy her one. She did not go out to play in the park as she was very sad. In the evening when it was time for her father to come back home, she was sitting next to the window. That day her father came late. By the time her father came she had gone to the bed to sleep. Suddenly there was a sound of the doorbell ringing. Her mother opened up the door. Karen got a surprise from her father. Her father had bought a new and a very beautiful doll for her.

12. **Why was Karen sad?**
    (a) Because she did not have friends.
    (b) She could not eat.
    (c) Her father did not buy a new doll for her.
    (d) She got hurt.

13. **Why didn't Karen go out to play?**
    (a) She was hurt.
    (b) She did not have a new doll to play.
    (c) There was no one in the park
    (d) Her mother did not let her go.

14. **When did her father come?**
    (a) When she was playing in the park.
    (b) When she had gone to sleep.
    (c) When she was sitting next to the window.
    (d) When she was crying .

15. **What is the synonym of beautiful?**

(a) Pretty   (b) Ugly   (c) Tall   (d) Strong

16. **What is the antonym of refused?**

(a) Agreed   (b) Believed   (c) Kind   (d) Honest

17. **If your father does not buy you anything what should you do?**

(a) Get angry with your parents

(b) Become sad.

(c) Force them to buy

(d) Try to understand and be happy with what you have.

Directions (Qs. 18–21): Read the poem given below and answer from the options given below.   (Tricky, 2014)

Let me fly

I am a bird

I fly high in the sky

Nothing but, I love to fly

I have my wings,

I love no other things

I just live to fly

Let me fly as high

I want to reach the sky

I want to touch it

To touch the moon

And the Sun

It's a great fun

I just love to fly

18. **What does the bird love to do?**

(a) It loves to eat grains.   (b) It loves to run

(c) It loves to play   (d) It loves to fly

19. **What does it want to touch?**

(a) The flowers   (b) The Sun and the Moon.

(c) The ground   (d) Its wings

20. **Where does it want to reach?**

    (a)   The mountains   (b)   The clouds

    (c)   The sky   (d)   The Sun

21. **Do you think that it would like to stay in a cage?**

    (a)   Yes, because it will get food there

    (b)   Yes, because it will get a house to live

    (c)   No, because it loves its freedom

    (d)   Yes, because it will play under no fear.

Directions (Qs. 22–27): Read the following passage and answer the questions from the options given below.   **(2016)**

HARD WORK PAYS

There was a small village named Pampu, in a faraway land. The people out there were very lazy. They would not get up early in the morning. They would sleep till late in the afternoon. They did not like to work hard. They always thought that something magical will happen and they would become rich. When it used to rain, they stayed back saying that "it's raining heavily, we can't go now, we'll get wet, let it get over". And in the summers, when it was sunny, they would find another excuse. They would do only the least, to survive. So they did not have any savings. All that was earned was so little that it could not be saved. Once there was a drought, the ground was all dry. Now there was no one, who had his savings. They all began to die, of thirst and hunger. They had been so lazy that they had not even dug a well. Within a few days, half the population had died of hunger and thirst. Whosoever was left now, decided to leave the village . They all decided to go to some other place. They started moving, they found a new village. In the other village people were hardworking. Despite drought they were not suffering. They had enough savings to save them from hunger. They had built reservoirs to store water. The villagers now learnt the importance of hard work. They promised to themselves that they will also work hard.

22. **The people in Pampu village were _____**

    (a)   very hardworking   (b)   lazy

    (c)   kind   (d)   happy

23. **What time did they get up every day?**

    (a)   Early in the morning   (b)   In the afternoon

    (c)   Never   (d)   In the evening

24. **Why didn't the villagers come out during rains?**

    (a)   Because of the fear of getting wet

    (b)   Because they wanted to play with water

    (c)   Because they wanted to go somewhere else

    (d)   Because God stopped them.

25. What happens in drought?

(a) People start running

(b) There's no rainfall

(c) Sun stops rising

(d) There's excess of rainfall

26. What is a reservoir?

(a) A tank made to store water

(b) A river

(c) A lake

(d) A pipe to spray water.

27. What do you learn from this story?

(a) We should sleep till late.

(b) We should migrate.

(c) We should make our own food.

(d) We should always work hard.

Directions (Qs. 28–30): Read the information given below and answer the questions from the options given below.

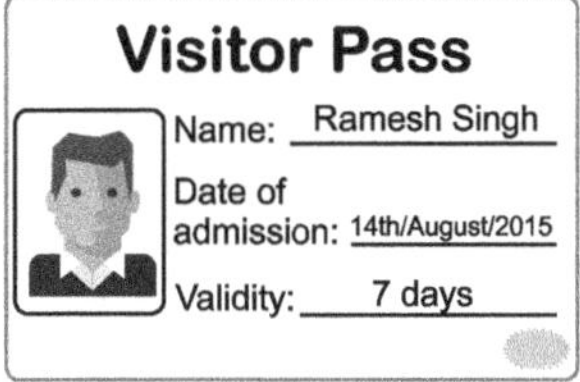

28. What is this ?

(a) In invitation card

(b) A pass

(c) A ticket

(d) A letter

29. How many people can use this card?

(a) Two   (b) Three   (c) One   (d) None

30. What are dates for which it is valid?

(a) 14th -20th August 2015.

(b) 13th-15th August, 2015

(c) 20th-24th September, 2014.

(d) 1st-13th July, 2013.

Read the passage and answer the questions that follow :   (2018)

Sanjay woke up early on Saturday and was very excited about the day ahead. He was going to go and play a cricket match with his team. It was his first cricket match, and he thought that they would win. The team had practiced a lot together and were ready. After he had breakfast, he got his cricket kit and then he went to meet his friends. Paul and Karim lived on the same street as Sanjay, and they were also in his team. The three boys walked to the cricket pitch in the centre of town. When they were on their way, the weather was good so they all thought that it would stay nice until they had finished. The three boys and the rest of the team went into the changing room to put on their cricket kits. When they were ready, they ran out onto the pitch and felt really confident about winning.

Example

The passage is about _______.

(a) Sanjay   (b) boys   **(c) cricket**   (d) weather

31. **Why was Sanjay excited ?**

Sanjay was excited about _________.

(a) the sunshine   (b) playing cricket

(c) meeting his friends   (d) winning

32. **How much did the team practice ?**

(a) Always   (b) Never   (c) Rarely   (d) A lot

33. **How was the weather ?**

(a) Wet   (b) Good   (c) Windy   (d) Hot

34. **Why did they go into the changing room ?**

(a) To talk   (b) To eat   (c) To change   (d) To run

For questions 35 to 39, read the passage and answer the questions that follow:
(2019)

Italy has a long history. After the Roman Empire broken down, there were many separate kingdoms and city states. Italy became one nation in 1861 and since then the country also includes the islands of Sicily and Sardegna. The 'Kingdom of Italy' lasted from 1861 until 1946. The Italian Republic was formed in 1946. Italy lies in Southern Europen and is one of the six founding countries of the European Union (EU). Italy borders six countries: France, Austria, Switzerland, Slovenia, Vatican City and San Marino.

Italy is easy to recognise on any world map, as the country is shaped like a high-heeled boot and it looks like it is kicking a ball, which is the island of Sicily. The country is slightly larger in size than the UK, the Netherlands and Belgium combined. This makes it the tenth largest country, just behind Poland, it terms of size and it is nearly 100 times bigger than the smallest European country.

Example

The passage is about _________.

(a) Sanjay   (b) boys   (c) Italy   (d) weather

35. **When did Italy first become one country ?**

(a) 3000   (b) 1946   (c) 1861   (d) 1941

36. What did Italy help to make ?

    (a) Rome   (b) The EU   (c) Sicily   (d) The Empire

37. How many countries have a border with Italy ?

    (a) Three   (b) Sixteen   (c) One   (d) Six

38. What does the island of Sicily look like on a map ?

    (a) A ball being kicked   (b) A shoe being worn

    (c) The UK   (d) Sardegna

39. How big is Italy ?

    (a) A little bit bigger than Poland

    (b) The biggest in Europe by a long way

    (c) The same as adding three other European countriesp

    (d) The smallest in Europe

Directions (Q. No. 40 and 44): The game of football was invented in the mid-19ᵗʰ century. In the year 1863, rugby football and association football branched off and Football Association in England was established. However, China claims to have played the first version of football centuries ago.

Both rugby football and association football were widely loved and played across the Atlantic. As rugby football came to be known as rugger and association football came to be known by the name, soccer in England, the Americans came up with their own version of the game and called it football.

Charles Goodyear designed and crafted the very first vulcanised rubber football in the year 1855. Most of the footballs are now being made with rubber bladders.

The first international association football match was played between Scotland and England in the year 1872. The match played by the national teams of England and Scotland was held at Scotland Cricket Club's ground located at Hamilton Crescent in Partick Scotland.

40. When was the game of football invented according to the passage?

        (2021)

    (a) In 1872   (b) In the mid-19ᵗʰ century

    (c) In 1855   (d) In 1863

41. Which of the following countries claims to have played the first version of football centuries ago? **(2021)**

    (a) England   (b) Scotland

    (c) America   (d) China

42. The first international association football match was played between _______

(2021)

(a) England and Scotland   (b) America and China

(c) China and Scotland   (d) England and China

43. When did Charles Goodyear design the first vulcanised rubber football?

(2021)

(a) In 1865   (b) In 1863

(c) In 1855   (d) In 1872

44. The association football later came to be known as _______ in England.

(2021)

(a) rugger   (b) soccer

(c) match   (d) rugby

Directions (Qs. 45-49): Read the passage and answer the questions that follow.

Long ago, in ancient times, a king had a large rock placed on a roadway. He then hid himself and watched to see if anyone would move the large rock out of the way. Some of the king's wealthiest merchants and courtiers came by and simply walked around it. Many people loudly blamed the king for not keeping the roads clear. But none of them did anything about getting the rock out of the way. A peasant then came along carrying a heavy load. Upon approaching the rock, he laid down his burden and tried to push it out of the road. After much pushing and heaving, he finally succeeded.

When the peasant went back to pick up his load, he noticed a purse lying on the road where the rock had been. The purse contained many gold coins and a note from the king explaining that the gold was for the person who removed the rock from the roadway.

45. Where did the king place the large rock?   (2022)

(a) Forest   (b) Roadway

(c) Palace   (d) Garden

46. The_______ and _______ came by and walked around the rock.   (2022)

(a) merchants, courtiers   (b) king, peasant

(c) merchants, king   (d) courtiers, peasant

47. In the given passage, who removed the rock lying on the road?   (2022)

(a) King   (b) Peasant

(c) Courtiers   (d) Merchants

48. What did the peasant find lying on the road?   (2022)

(a) A purse   (b) More stones

(c) A box   (d) A stick

49. Find the word from the passage which means the same as 'earliest'.

(2022)

(a) Burden   (b) Roadway
(c) Ancient   (d) Peasant

Direction for Q. No. 50 to 52: Read the passage given below and answer the questions that follow:

Early rising is a healthy habit. The morning air refreshes our body and mind. In the morning, our mind is fresh and energetic, so we can do any work with full concentration. When we get up early, we have more time to finish our work. Early rising improves our productivity and helps us to finish our work on time. The person who rises early in the morning gets more time to exercise. Exercise helps us to remain fit and healthy. One can witness the charm of nature in the early morning. There's a famous saying, "Early to bed and early to rise, makes a man healthy, wealthy and wise".

50. In the morning, our mind is: **(2022)**
    (a) fresh and energetic
    (b) lazy and energetic
    (c) fresh and dull
    (d) None of these

51. Which one of the following statements is incorrect according to the passage?

(2022)

    (a) Early rising is a healthy habit.
    (b) Early rising can damage our productivity.
    (c) Exercise helps us to remain fit and healthy.
    (d) The morning air refreshes our body and mind.

52. What is the same meaning of the word 'Refresh' used in the passage?
(2022)

(a) Hurt   (b) Sleepy
(c) Agitate   (d) Enliven

Direction for Q. No. 53 and 54: Arrange P, Q, R and S to make meaningful sentences:

53. with P he went Q his friends R to movie 5. **(2022)**
    P Q R S
(a) SQPR   (b) PRSQ
(c) QSPR   (d) QRSP

54. tries P something better Q to do R he always 5.   **(2022)**

P Q R S

(a) PQRS   (b) PSQR

(c) SQRP   (d) SPRQ

RESPONSE GRID

LEVEL 1

1. a b c d   2. a b c d   3. a b c d   4. a b c d   5. a b c d
6. a b c d   7. a b c d   8. a b c d   9. a b c d   10. a b c d
11. a b c d   12. a b c d   13. a b c d   14. a b c d   15. a b c d
16. a b c d   17. a b c d   18. a b c d   19. a b c d   20. a b c d
21. a b c d   22. a b c d   23. a b c d   24. a b c d   25. a b c d

LEVEL 2

1. a b c d   2. a b c d   3. a b c d   4. a b c d   5. a b c d
6. a b c d   7. a b c d   8. a b c d   9. a b c d   10. a b c d
11. a b c d   12. a b c d   13. a b c d   14. a b c d   15. a b c d
16. a b c d   17. a b c d   18. a b c d   19. a b c d   20. a b c d
21. a b c d   22. a b c d   23. a b c d   24. a b c d   25. a b c d
26. a b c d   27. a b c d   28. a b c d   29. a b c d   30. a b c d
31. a b c d   32. a b c d   33. a b c d   34. a b c d   35. a b c d
36. a b c d   37. a b c d   38. a b c d   39. a b c d   40. a b c d
41. a b c d   42. a b c d   43. a b c d   44. a b c d   45. a b c d
46. a b c d   47. a b c d   48. a b c d   49. a b c d   50. a b c d
51. a b c d   52. a b c d   53. a b c d   54. a b c d

Solutions with Explanation

LEVEL - 1

1. **(c)** Because his father was taking him out for picnic.
2. **(c)** Deer park

3. **(b)** Five
4. **(a)** Outdoor games
5. **(b)** small. (Antonyms are opposite words)
6. **(c)** Money given on Eid.
7. **(c)** To enjoy with friends.
8. **(a)** a different way
9. **(b)** the sweets made by his mother
10. **(d)** in doing some noble work
11. **(c)** small   12. **(b)** long
13. **(b)** white   14. **(b)** fresh
15. **(c)** fast   16. **(d)** Delicious food
17. **(d)** The wise men of his kingdom
18. **(c)** A group of boys
19. **(b)** Working in their farm.
20. **(b)** Because they were working together
21. (c) Lhasa
22. (b) south
23. (c) it is protected by mountain barriers from monsoon
24. (c) there is limited arable land
25. (c) potatoes

LEVEL – 2

1. **(b)** shrewd person   2. **(b)** Lend money
3. **(b)** Double   4. **(c)** Borrow
5. **(b)** He had to work for the rich man.   6. **(a)** Because it is scared of it.
7. **(c)** In a hole   8. **(d)** Outside the hole
9. **(a)** Peal   10. **(b)** It will eat the mouse.
11. **(d)** All of the above, because the cat will eat the mouse, the mouse will be scared of the cat. and also because cat's favorite food is a mouse
12. **(c)** Her father did not buy a new doll for her.
13. **(b)** She did not have a new doll to play. .
14. **(b)** When she had gone to sleep.
15. **(a)** Pretty. Synonyms are words that have similar meanings
16. **(a)** Agreed. Antonyms are words that have opposite meanings.
17. **(d)** Try to understand and be happy with what you have
18. **(d)** It loves to fly.

19. **(b)** The Sun and the Moon.

20. **(c)** The sky

21. **(c)** No, because it loves its freedom

22. **(b)** lazy

23. **(b)** In the afternoon

24. **(a)** Because of the fear of getting wet.

25. **(b)** There's no rainfall. Drought is a condition when there is no rainfall and hence no crops can be grown.

26. **(a)** A tank made to store water.

27. **(d)** We should always work hard.

28. **(b)** A pass.

29. **(c)** One

30. **(a)** 14th-20th August 2015.

31. **(b)** playing cricket   32. **(d)**   A lot

33. **(b)** Good   34. **(c)**   To change

35. **(c)** 1861   36. **(b)**   The EU

37. **(d)** Six   38. **(a)**   A ball being kicked

39. **(c)** The same as adding three other European countries

40. **(b)** The game of football was invented mid 19th century.

41. **(d)** China claims to have played the first version of football.

42. **(a)** England and Scotland played the first international association football match.

43. **(c)** In 1855, Charles Goodyear designed the first vulcanised rubber football.

44. **(b)** Soccer is the new name for association football.

45. **(b)** The king placed the big rock on the roadway.

46. **(a)** The merchants and courtiers came by and walked around the rock.

47. **(b)** The Peasant removed the rock lying on the road.

48. **(a)** The Peasant found the purse lying on the road, after removing the big Rock.

49. **(c)** Ancient means Earliest.

50. **(a)** 51. **(b)**   52. **(d)**   53. **(c)**   54. **(d)**

16
Chapter

Spell-B

It is necessary and also interesting to learn spellings as they form the base of any language. To be a high achiever in this section, students need to increase their vocabulary with correctly spelt words.

The best way to improve your spellings is to practise reading and writing with their correct spellings. If a student reads incorrect spellings, he gets exposure to these misspelt words and his mind learns the incorrect spellings. In this way whenever he writes in future, he makes mistakes in spelling. The learning process of an individual requires the involvement of several senses to learn quickly and in a better way. The individual should be familiar with his weak areas of spellings so as to work on those. The individual should be well aware about the affixes so that he can organize the words and is able to form relevant associations. The next way to improve one's spellings and vocabulary is to bring the words in daily use so that one becomes familiar with the particular words. In case an individual is facing difficulty in learning some words, he can make a list of such words, learn these spellings and frequently use them while speaking and writing.

Group learning is better than solo learning. Individuals in a group ask one another various questions concerning different things, persons and other ideas and practise using new words in such interaction. Thus, they acquire many words without putting much effort in learning them. Group discussion is the most appropriate way to learn one word substitution quickly.

This chapter will help you to:

- Find the correctly spelt word out of incorrectly spelled words.
- Use one word replacing a sentence.
- Fill the letters which are left out to complete the word.

Based on spelling, there are three sets of question in the Olympiad question paper. (i) The first set contains 4 different words having one of them spelled correctly, and the rest of them are incorrectly spelled.

For example:

1. (a) tomoro   (b)   motivet   (c)   computer   (d)   fabulus

2. (a) defeat   (b) intellegent   (c) eliphant   (d) fluor

If one is aware of the correct spelling of all these words, one can easily make out that '(c) computer' and '(a) defeat' are the only words which have been spelled correctly in this set. Hence '(c) computer' and "(a) defeat should be marked as the answer.

(ii) The second set contains the same word spelled in 4 various ways; one out of them is the correct spelling of the said word.

For example:

   (a) mountain   (b)   mounten   (c)   montain   (d)   maunten

   (b) prezedent (b)   hungary   (c)   tortoise   (d)   bergar

For the student who is familiar with the correct spelling of these words, there would be no hitch in choosing '(a) mountain' and '(c) tortoise' as the right answer.

(iii) The third set contains only one word in which some blank spaces are provided to insert the right letter(s) taken from the options given.

For example:

1. ext – m -- ly

   (a) i,e   (b)   e,i   (c)   a,i   (d)   e,e

2. tu – t – e

   (a) l,r   (b)   l,e   (c)   u,r   (d)   r,l

One who is acquainted with the given words would not hesitate to state that '(d) e,e' and '(d) r,l are the right options because missing places in the first word given requires 'e' at both the blank spaces to make the word 'extremely' while in the second r,l is required to make the word 'turtle.'

Multiple Choice Questions

(Directions for questions 1–20): Choose the correctly spelt word.

1.	(a) manth	(b) dey	(c) iear	(d) week
2.	(a) schul	(b) doeg	(c) garden	(d) cheir
3.	(a) flewer	(b) cards	(c) staps	(d) sihp
4.	(a) lion	(b) eliphant	(c) stoodents	(d) palayer
5.	(a) mankey	(b) bird	(c) baux	(d) indea
6.	(a) animel	(b) peple	(c) fish	(d) riever
7.	(a) montain	(b) valliys	(c) beilding	(d) palace
8.	(a) wolf	(b) kniphe	(c) banch	(d) brus
9.	(a) babie	(b) salt	(c) suger	(d) saend
10.	(a) mathar	(b) douter	(c) sister	(d) aanti
11.	(a) ankal	(b) bruthur	(c) fadar	(d) son
12.	(a) computer	(b) paen	(c) rabbur	(d) buk
13.	(a) crickett	(b) ball	(c) trackc	(d) halicoptre
14.	(a) hokey	(b) talevison	(c) bicycle	(d) scuter
15.	(a) trea	(b) rean	(c) pakr	(d) umbrella
16.	(a) rainbow	(b) corton	(c) haspitel	(d) hotal
17.	(a) garl	(b) creeper	(c) claimber	(d) plent
18.	(a) paiano	(b) tannis	(c) golf	(d) leptoup
19.	(a) aple	(b) tiger	(c) gaet	(d) leapord
20.	(a) shue	(b) shart	(c) socks	(d) wach

(Directions for question 21–40): select the word which is not misspelt.

21.	(a) kenel	(b) kennal	(c) kanal	(d) kennel
22.	(a) anser	(b) ansor	(c) answer	(d) answor
23.	(a) tution	(b) tuition	(c) tuson	(d) tusion
24.	(a) complete	(b) complit	(c) comlite	(d) cumplete
25.	(a) pasent	(b) patient	(c) pasant	(d) paseant
26.	(a) sadenly	(b) sudenly	(c) suddenly	(d) sudenly
27.	(a) sentance	(b) santance	(c) santans	(d) sentence
28.	(a) juice	(b) juse	(c) juce	(d) joose
29.	(a) carten	(b) curtain	(c) curten	(d) cartan
30.	(a) becos	(b) becous	(c) because	(d) beacaus
31.	(a) berthday	(b) burthday	(c) barthday	(d) birthday

32.	(a) popular	(b) pouplar	(c) popler	(d) poupler
33.	(a) frend	(b) friend	(c) frand	(d) fraind
34.	(a) cuntrey	(b) cauntry	(c) country	(d) cuntrey
35.	(a) tortaise	(b) taurtaise	(c) tourtoise	(d) tortoise
36.	(a) rainbow	(b) renbo	(c) ranbou	(d) rainbeau
37.	(a) paulite	(b) polite	(c) polaite	(d) poulite
38.	(a) soulder	(b) sollder	(c) soldier	(d) solger
39.	(a) laibrari	(b) laibrary	(c) libray	(d) library
40.	(a) teacher	(b) techer	(c) taecher	(d) tacher

(Directions for Questions 41–50): Select the word which can be replaced for the given sentence.

41. **A place where patients are treated for their ailments ----------**
    (a) Park   (b) hospital   (c) hotel   (d) club

42. **A place where tigers live -------------**
    (a) burrow   (b) hole   (c) den   (d) nest

43. **A person who makes ornaments with gold ----------------**
    (a) blacksmith   (b) plumber   (c) goldsmith   (d) labourer

44. **A heavenly body that changes its shape everyday ------------------**
    (a) moon   (b) star   (c) earth   (d) sun

45. **One of the greatest wonders of the world ------------------**
    (a) Rashtrapati Bhavan   (b) Qutub Minar
    (c) Red Fort   (d) Taj Mahal

46. **A person who plays cricket -----------------------**
    (a) cricketer   (b) athlete   (c) sprinter   (d) boxer

47. **Horses live in a --------------**
    (a) cowshed   (b) kennel   (c) stable   (d) den

48. **A tool for fixing a nail into the wall ---------------------**
    (a) screw driver   (b) hammer   (c) plier   (d) axe

49. **A musical instrument made out of bamboo ----------------**
    (a) harmonium   (b) guitar   (c) flute   (d) whistle

50. **A person who rings the bell in a school --------------**
    (a) peon   (b) librarian   (c) clerk   (d) maid

(Directions for questions 51–60)   Fill in the blanks with the suitable pair of alphabets provided as the option to make a meaningful word

51. **w – m – n**
    (a) a,o   (b) u,o   (c) e,o   (d) o,a

52. **co – pu – er**
    (a) t,m   (b) m,t   (c) n,t   (d) t,n
53. **dau -- -- ter**
    (a) c,h   (b) e,j   (c) g,h   (d) h,g
54. **sc – ot – r**
    (a) e,o   (b) o,e   (c) u,e   (d) e,u
55. **he – icop – er**
    (a) l,t   (b) k,t   (c) u,t   (d) e,t
56. **swe – t –r**
    (a) e,a   (b) i,e   (c) a,e   (d) u,e
57. **c -- -- f**
    (a) e,l   (b) a,l   (c) o,l   (d) u,l
58. **mus -- -- m**
    (a) u,e   (b) i,u   (c) e,u   (d) a,u
59. **bru -- --**
    (a) s,e   (b) c,h   (c) c,s   (d) s,h
60. **bad – in – on**
    (a) t,m   (b) m,t   (c) e,m   (d) m,e

Directions (Q. 61 and 63): Choose the word which is spelled correctly.

61. ___________   (2020)
    (a) Category
    (b) Ketegury
    (c) Cetegury
    (d) Catagory

Example
    (a) Acek
    (b) Cake
    (c) Kace
    (d) Caek

62. ___________   (2020)
    (a) Curancy   (b) Curransy   (c) Curerancy   (d) Currency
63. ___________   (2020)
    (a) Superority   (b) Supreirity   (c) Supreoirty   (d) Superiority

Directions (Q. 64): Choose the word which is spelled correctly.   (2021)
Example
    (a) Acek   (b) Cake   (b) Kace   (d) Caek
64. (a) Elegant   (b) Eligent   (c) Iligant   (d) Elegent

Directions (Q. 65 and 66): Choose the word which is spelled correctly.   (2022)
65. (a) Waitar   (b) Waetar   (c) Walter   (d) Weiter
66. (a) Toruble   (b) Truble   (c) Trabel   (d) Trouble
67. **Identify the correctly spelt word.**   (2022)
    (a) Attempt   (b) Atempt   (c) Attampt   (d) Attempet

68. Choose the word which is spelled correctly.   **(2021)**

   (a)   Accomodate   (b)   Acommodate   (c)   Accommodate   (d)   Acomodate

69. Choose the word which is SPELLED correctly.   **(2022)**

   (a)   Jiantic   (b)   Gijantic   (c)   Giantik   (d)   Gigantic

RESPONSE GRID

1. a b c d	2. a b c d	3. a b c d	4. a b c d	5. a b c d
6. a b c d	7. a b c d	8. a b c d	9. a b c d	10. a b c d
11. a b c d	12. a b c d	13. a b c d	14. a b c d	15. a b c d
16. a b c d	17. a b c d	18. a b c d	19. a b c d	20. a b c d
21. a b c d	22. a b c d	23. a b c d	24. a b c d	25. a b c d
26. a b c d	27. a b c d	28. a b c d	29. a b c d	30. a b c d
31. a b c d	32. a b c d	33. a b c d	34. a b c d	35. a b c d
36. a b c d	37. a b c d	38. a b c d	39. a b c d	40. a b c d
41. a b c d	42. a b c d	43. a b c d	44. a b c d	45. a b c d
46. a b c d	47. a b c d	48. a b c d	49. a b c d	50. a b c d
51. a b c d	52. a b c d	53. a b c d	54. a b c d	55. a b c d
56. a b c d	57. a b c d	58. a b c d	59. a b c d	60. a b c d
61. a b c d	62. a b c d	63. a b c d	64. a b c d	65. a b c d
66. a b c d	67. a b c d	68. a b c d	69. a b c d	

Solutions with Explanation

1. (d)	2. (c)	3. (b)	4. (a)	5. (b)	6. (c)	7. (d)	8. (a)
9. (b)	10. (c)	11. (d)	12. (a)	13. (b)	14. (c)	15. (d)	16. (a)
17. (b)	18. (c)	19. (b)	20. (c)	21. (d)	22. (c)	23. (b)	24. (a)
25. (b)	26. (c)	27. (d)	28. (a)	29. (b)	30. (c)	31. (d)	32. (a)
33. (b)	34. (c)	35. (d)	36. (a)	37. (b)	38. (c)	39. (d)	40. (a)

41. (b) hospital   **42.** (c) den   **43.** (c) goldsmith   **44.** (a) moon

45. (d) Taj Mahal   **46.** (a) cricketer   **47.** (c) stable   **48.** (b) hammer

49. (c) flute   **50.** (a) peon

51. (d)   **52.** (b)   **53.** (c)   **54.** (b)   **55.** (a)   **56.** (c)   **57.** (b)   **58.** (c)

59. (d)   **60.** (b)

61. (a) Category   **62.** (d) Currency   **63.** (d) Superiority

64. (a) Elegant is the correct spelling.   **65.** (c) Waiter is the correct spelling.

66. (d) Trouble is the correct spelling in the following case.

67. (a)

68. (c) Accommodate is the correct spelling.

69. (d) The only correct spelling is Gigantic.